Lucky Charm
QUILTS

17 Delightful Patterns for Precut 5" Squares

Compiled by Lissa Alexander

Moda All-Stars
Lucky Charm Quilts:
17 Delightful Patterns for Precut 5" Squares
© 2017 by Martingale & Company®

Martingale®
19021 120th Ave. NE, Ste. 102
Bothell, WA 98011-9511 USA
ShopMartingale.com

Printed in China
22 21 20 19 18   8 7 6 5 4 3 2

Library of Congress Cataloging-in-Publication Data
is available upon request.

ISBN: 978-1-60468-846-7

MISSION STATEMENT

We empower makers who use fabric and yarn
to make life more enjoyable.

CREDITS

PUBLISHER AND
CHIEF VISIONARY OFFICER
Jennifer Erbe Keltner

CONTENT DIRECTOR
Karen Costello Soltys

DESIGN MANAGER
Adrienne Smitke

MANAGING EDITOR
Tina Cook

PRODUCTION MANAGER
Regina Girard

ACQUISITIONS EDITOR
Karen M. Burns

COVER DESIGNER
Elizabeth Stumbo

TECHNICAL EDITOR
Beth Bradley

PHOTOGRAPHER
Brent Kane

COPY EDITOR
Durby Peterson

ILLUSTRATOR
Christine Erikson

SPECIAL THANKS

Thanks to Suzie and Bernhard Bauer of Snohomish, Washington, and Lynn Austin of Kirkland, Washington, for allowing the photography for this book to take place in their homes.

Contents

Introduction

Everyone loves a charm pack. *What quilter can resist the delightful little bundles of 5" squares that include at least one square (sometimes two!) of every fabric in a collection? Shops often keep these impulse-worthy bundles near the checkout stand. It's so easy to toss another charm pack on the pile!*

But let's be real. Sometimes our enthusiasm to acquire outpaces our plan to sew these little bundles. What to do? Stop collecting? Never! It's time to turn those charm squares into fabulous quilts.

You're in luck! Enter the talented, creative, and always-charming Moda All-Stars designers. This time, they've got you covered with projects as easy as 1, 2, 3—one, two, or three charm packs, that is! Every project in this book begins with charm packs. Add some background fabric and you're all set.

And best of all, know that your purchase of this book makes you a lucky charm, of sorts, for children with cancer. All royalties for the book are being donated to Alex's Lemonade Stand Foundation (AlexsLemonade.org), an organization dedicated to raising funds for research into new treatments and cures for all children battling cancer. Together, let's do good and quilt an end to this disease forever.

~Lissa Alexander

Teatime Quilt by Laurie Simpson

- **FINISHED QUILT:** 21¾" × 26¾"
- **FINISHED BLOCKS:** 3¾" × 3¾" and 3¾" × 5"
- **CHARM PACKS NEEDED:** ■ □ □

Dress up a table or wall with a cheerful checkered quilt in a classic combination of red, cream, and blue. Use a charm pack that includes a variety of red on cream prints to add a scrappy touch.

Materials

Yardage is based on 42"-wide fabric. Charm squares are 5" × 5".

32 cream print charm squares for blocks
3 red print charm squares for accent squares
⅔ yard of red print for blocks and binding
¼ yard of blue plaid linen/cotton for rectangles*
⅔ yard of fabric for backing
26" × 31" piece of batting

*Depending on your fabric, more yardage might be needed to fussy-cut the rectangles to center the plaid motif.

Cutting

All measurements include ¼"-wide seam allowances.

From *each* cream print charm square, cut:
2 strips, 1¾" × 5" (64 total)

From *each* red print charm square, cut:
1 square, 4¼" × 4¼" (3 total)

From the red print for blocks and binding, cut:
3 strips, 5" × 42"; crosscut the strips into 65 strips,
    1¾" × 5"
3 strips, 2" × 42"*

*Feel free to cut wider binding strips if desired.

Continued on page 8

Charmed, I'm Sure!

from **LAURIE SIMPSON**

If Laurie Simpson's charm oozed out in colors, it would be red, white, and blue all over! She's the quilty half of the Minick and Simpson fabric design team (MinickandSimpson.blogspot.com).

- **What charms me most about charm packs is** rifling through them like a deck of cards. It's fabric magic!

- **Same or different? If you're making a project with multiple charm packs, are you more likely to use two or three from the same collection or from different collections?** Always different. The more the merrier.

- **This works like a charm for me every time:** Starching the fabric and, if the pattern allows it, trimming the pinked edges.

- **About those pinked edges, here's my advice for taking them into account when you sew:** If possible, I trim them. If the pattern calls for a full 5" square, then I close my eyes and wing it.

- **Besides a 5" charm-square, my other go-to precut shape is** a fat quarter.

- **If I taught at Quilters' Finishing School, I'd teach the students to** hand quilt—preferably with your feet up, sitting in a comfy chair, and watching something nice on TV.

- **If I had to pick a "lucky" charm out of a charm pack, I'd choose one that** was either red, white, or blue.

Continued from page 7

From the blue plaid, cut:

6 rectangles, 4¼" × 5½"**

**Laurie fussy-cut the blue plaid, centering the intersecting blue lines in each rectangle.*

Assembling the Blocks

Press the seam allowances as indicated by the arrows.

1 Sew one cream strip between two red strips to make strip set A. Make 22. From each strip set, crosscut two 1¾"-wide segments for a total of 44 A segments.

Strip set A.
Make 22. Cut 44 segments, 1¾" × 4¼".

2 Sew one red strip between two cream strips to make strip set B. Make 21. From each strip set, crosscut two 1¾"-wide segments for a total of 42 B segments.

Strip set B.
Make 21. Cut 42 segments, 1¾" × 4¼".

3 To make block A, arrange two A segments and one B segment in three rows as shown. Join the rows. Make 10 A blocks measuring 4¼" square.

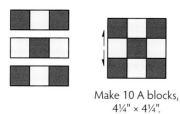

Make 10 A blocks,
4¼" × 4¼".

4 To make block B, arrange two B segments and one A segment in three rows as shown. Join the rows. Make eight B blocks measuring 4¼" square.

Make 8 B blocks,
4¼" × 4¼".

5 To make block C, arrange two A segments and two B segments in four rows as shown. Join the rows. Make eight C blocks measuring 4¼" × 5½".

Make 8 C blocks,
4¼" × 5½".

Assembling the Quilt

Press the seam allowances as indicated by the arrows. Lay out the A, B, and C blocks with the red squares and plaid rectangles in seven rows as shown. Join the units in each row, and then join the rows. The quilt should measure 21¾" × 26¾".

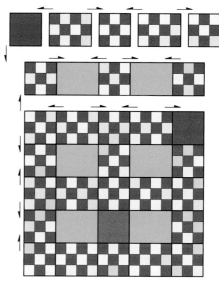

Quilt assembly

Finishing the Quilt

Go to ShopMartingale.com/HowtoQuilt for more details on quilting and finishing.

1 Layer the backing, batting, and quilt top; baste the layers together. Quilt as desired. The quilt shown was hand quilted in diagonal parallel lines placed 1¾" apart.

2 Use the red 2"-wide strips to make the binding and attach it to the quilt.

Forever Friends *by Lisa Bongean*

- **FINISHED QUILTS:** 17" square each
- **FINISHED BLOCK:** 3" × 3"
- **CHARM PACKS NEEDED:** ■ □ □

Just one charm pack is all it takes to make a pair of coordinating mini-quilts—one to keep and one to give to a treasured friend. Embellish the corner of the quilt with a touch of wool appliqué and a sweet embroidered sentiment.

Materials

The supplies listed are enough to make 2 mini-quilts. Yardage is based on 42"-wide fabric. Charm squares are 5" × 5".

1 charm pack of tan, brown, and red prints for blocks (you'll need 18 tan, 10 brown, and 9 red squares)
1 yard of tan solid for blocks, sashing, border, and binding
1 square, 5" × 5", of red wool for appliqué
⅝ yard of fabric for backing
2 squares, 21" × 21", of batting
Primitive Gatherings ¾" half-square-triangle charm paper*
Removable fabric marker
Fusible web (such as Lite Steam-A-Seam 2)
Coordinating pearl cotton and chenille needle for appliqué and embroidery

* This piecing paper is designed to efficiently and accurately make 18 tiny half-square-triangle units from charm squares.

Cutting

All measurements include ¼"-wide seam allowances.

From 1 of the brown charm squares, cut:
8 squares, 1¼" × 1¼"

Continued on page 12

Continued from page 11

From the tan solid, cut:

3 strips, 3½" × 42"; crosscut into:

    4 strips, 3½" × 17"

    4 strips, 3½" × 11"

    24 rectangles, 1¼" × 3½"

4 strips, 1¼" × 42"*

*Lisa used 1¼"-wide strips to make a single-fold binding that fits the small scale of the quilts, but cut 2½"-wide strips if you prefer a double-fold binding.

Assembling the Blocks

Press the seam allowances as indicated by the arrows. Each block is made from one dark (red or brown) charm square and one tan charm square. Select nine red and nine brown charm squares. Pair each dark square with one tan square for a total of 18 pairs.

1 Place one dark and one tan square right sides together with the tan square on top. Center one triangle piecing paper on the tan square. Shorten the machine stitch length to approximately 1 mm. Sew along the marked lines on the piecing paper as indicated by the manufacturer's instructions.

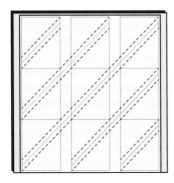

2 Cut through the layers along all of the solid lines as indicated by the manufacturer's instructions. With the paper still in place, press the seam allowances of each half-square triangle. Remove the paper from each unit by bending it away from the fabric and then pulling it from the center close to the seam. Trim away the dog-ears. Each charm square pair will yield 18 half-square-triangle units that are 1¼" square, including seam allowances; 16 are needed for each block.

Make 18 units,
1¼" × 1¼", from each pair.

3 Lay out 16 matching half-square-triangle units in four rows of four as shown. Join the units in each row, and then join the rows. The block should measure 3½" square. Make nine brown blocks and nine red blocks.

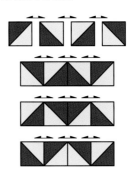
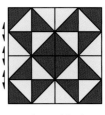

Make 18 blocks,
3½" × 3½".

Assembling the Quilt Tops

Press the seam allowances as indicated by the arrows.

1 Lay out the blocks for each quilt top in three rows of three, alternating the brown and red blocks as shown. One quilt top will have four red and five brown blocks, and the other will have five red blocks and four brown blocks.

Charmed, I'm Sure!

from **LISA BONGEAN**

Lisa Bongean (LisaBongean.com) packs a whole lot of charm into little bitty pieces with her signature patchwork style. She's both the brains and the beauty behind the Primitive Gatherings fabric line.

- **What charms me most about charm packs is** that these little goodies make it possible to collect every fabric from all my favorite lines!

- **Same or different? If you're making a project with multiple charm packs are you more likely to use two or three from the same collection or from different collections?** Different.

- **This works like a charm for me every time:** Can I say looming deadline? No . . . lol! When I use charms, I am usually making small quilts. Pressing seam allowances open makes a huge difference in accuracy when piecing is little, along with a lot of starch.

- **About those pinked edges, here's my advice for taking them into account when you sew:** Rarely do I use the whole 5" charm as is, so those edges don't bother me at all!

- **Besides a 5" charm-square, my other go-to precut shape is** a fat quarter.

- **If I taught at Quilters' Finishing School, I'd teach the students to** put a sleeve on every quilt. What seems like a utilitarian quilt to some may be wall art to another; hanging sleeves are amazing for displaying quilts.

- **If I had to pick a "lucky" charm out of a charm pack, I'd choose** one that has a tiny print. I love tiny prints, the smaller the better.

- **In Charm School, you learn the social graces. But in Quilter's Charm School you learn** that great things can happen when you team up with another person. Connecting is priceless and important to our well-being. So, in other words, something as small as one single charm paired with a background can turn into a whole quilt block!

2 Place a tan 1¼" × 3½" rectangle between the blocks in each row. For the two sashing rows in each quilt, lay out three tan 1¼" × 3½" rectangles alternating with two brown squares as shown in the quilt assembly diagram. Join the units in each row, and then join the rows. Each quilt center should measure 11" square.

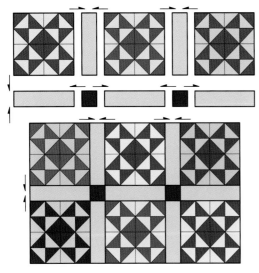

Quilt assembly

3 Sew the tan 3½" × 11" border strips to the sides of each quilt top; press the seam allowances toward the border. Sew the 3½" × 17" strips to the top and bottom of each quilt top; press. Each quilt top should measure 17" square.

Embellishing the Quilts

1 Use a removable fabric marker and light box or your preferred transfer method to trace the *forever friends* embroidery design on page 15 onto each bottom border, referring to the photo on page 11 for placement. Embroider the design using a chenille needle, pearl cotton, and the stem stitch.

2 Trace the heart template on page 15 twice onto the paper side of a piece of fusible web. Fuse the web to the wrong side of the wool square, and then cut out two hearts along the drawn lines. Remove the paper backing, and then fuse one heart to each quilt, referring to the photo for placement. Hand stitch the edge of each heart using pearl cotton and a blanket stitch or whipstitch.

Finishing the Quilts

Go to ShopMartingale.com/HowtoQuilt for more details on quilting and finishing.

1 Layer the backing, batting, and quilt top; baste the layers together. Hand or machine quilt as desired. The quilts shown were machine quilted in the ditch, by Valerie Krueger, to outline the shapes of the blocks. The borders were quilted with large curving feathers and parallel lines.

2 Use the tan 1¼"-wide strips to make single-fold binding and attach it to the quilts.

Heart
Cut 2 from red wool.

Appliqué patterns do not include seam allowances.

Simply Charmed by Sherri McConnell

- FINISHED TABLE RUNNER: 16½" × 40½"
- FINISHED BLOCK: 4" × 4"
- CHARM PACKS NEEDED: ■ ☐ ☐

Make a quick and easy table runner using exactly 40 charm squares. Basic half-square triangles are all you need to create the striking diagonal striped design.

Materials

Yardage is based on 42"-wide fabric. Charm squares are 5" × 5".

1 charm pack of assorted navy, yellow, orange, teal, tan, and cream prints for quilt top (you'll need 20 light and 20 dark squares)

¼ yard of navy print for binding

1⅓ yards of fabric for backing

21" × 45" piece of batting

Cutting

All measurements include ¼"-wide seam allowances.

From the navy print for binding, cut:

3 strips, 2½" × 42"

Charmed, I'm Sure!

from **SHERRI McCONNELL**

Sherri McConnell leads a charmed life—a charmed quilting life, that is (aQuiltingLife.com).

- **What charms me most about charm packs is** that they're a terrific way to sample every piece of a collection, and they're perfect for scrap quilts!

- **Same or different? If you're making a project with multiple charm packs, are you more likely to use two or three from the same collection or from different collections?** Different.

- **About those pinked edges, here's my advice for taking them into account when you sew:** I use the outer part of the pinked edge as the outer edge of the fabric.

- **Besides a 5" charm-square, my other go-to precut shape is** a 2½" strip.

- **If I taught at Quilters' Finishing School, I'd teach the students to** press binding away from the quilt front after machine stitching and before hand stitching it to the back.

- **If I had to pick a "lucky" charm out of a charm pack, I'd choose** one that's blue, if possible, with a large floral or small geometric print.

- **In Charm School, you learn the social graces. But in Quilter's Charm School you learn that** there is a low-volume background to complement every charm square.

Assembling the Half-Square-Triangle Units

Press the seam allowances as indicated by the arrows.

1 Organize the charm squares into 20 light/dark pairs. Make sure there is a high contrast in the light and dark values of the two squares in each pair. Draw a diagonal line from corner to corner on the wrong side of the light squares.

2 Place one pair of squares right sides together with the light square on top. Sew ¼" from each side of the drawn line. Cut along the line to yield two half-square-triangle units. Press and trim the units to measure 4½" square. Make 40 half-square-triangle units.

Make 40.

LIKE A CHARM

"Pressing half-square-triangle seam allowances open works like a charm for me every time."
~Sherri

Assembling the Table Runner

Press the seam allowances as indicated by the arrows. Lay out the half-square-triangle units in four rows of 10, orienting them as shown to create a diagonal striped pattern. Join the units in each row, and then join the rows. The runner top should be 16½" × 40½".

Finishing the Table Runner

Go to ShopMartingale.com/HowtoQuilt for more details on quilting and finishing.

1 Layer the backing, batting, and runner top; baste the layers together. Hand or machine quilt as desired. The table runner shown was machine quilted with an allover swirl and feather design.

2 Use the navy 2½"-wide strips to make the binding and attach it to the runner.

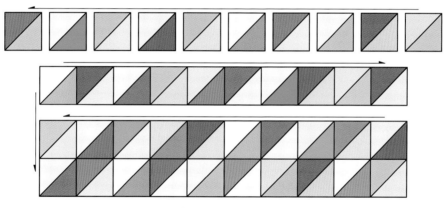

Table-runner assembly

Holiday Charm

by **Lynne Hagmeier**

Pieced and quilted by Lois Sprecker

- **FINISHED TABLE RUNNER: 16½" × 32½"**
- **FINISHED BLOCK: 4" × 4"**
- **CHARM PACKS NEEDED:** ■ □ □

Decorate the table for the holidays with an elegant embellished table runner with accents of rich red, gold, and green. Lynne's clever layered patchwork technique will save you time when appliquéing the blocks.

Materials

Yardage is based on 42"-wide fabric. Charm squares are 5" × 5".

1 charm pack of assorted prints for blocks (11 tan and 21 dark red, gold, black, and green squares)
½ yard of black print for border and binding
⅝ yard of fabric for backing
21" × 37" piece of batting
Fusible web
Glue stick
10 black buttons, ½"-diameter

Cutting

All measurements include ¼"-wide seam allowances.

From *each* of 11 tan charm squares, cut:

2 squares, 2½" × 2½"; cut each square in half
    diagonally to yield 2 triangles (44 total)*

From *each* of 21 dark charm squares, cut:

1 square, 4½" × 4½" (21 total)

From the black print, cut:

6 strips, 2½" × 42"; crosscut *3 of the strips* into:
    2 strips, 2½" × 28½"
    2 strips, 2½" × 16½"

**Refer to the cutting diagram below to retain the
rectangles remaining from 10 charm squares for petal
appliqués. (See "Appliquéing the Blocks" below for
directions on preparing and cutting the petals.)*

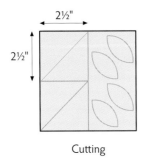

Cutting

Appliquéing the Blocks

1 Use the remaining rectangles from 10 of the tan
charm squares to make the petals for the Four-Petal
blocks. Using the pattern on page 24, trace four petals
onto the paper side of a piece of fusible web. Fuse the
fusible web to the wrong side of one tan rectangle. Cut

four petals along the drawn lines. Repeat to make 10
sets of four matching petals.

2 Select 10 dark squares for the backgrounds of the
Four-Petal blocks. Center four matching petals
right side up on one dark square as shown. Fuse the
petals in place. Topstitch each petal ⅛" from the raw
edge. Make 10.

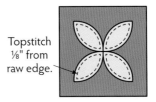

Topstitch
⅛" from
raw edge.

Make 10 blocks,
4½" × 4½".

3 Select 11 dark squares for the backgrounds of the
Square in a Square blocks. Pair each dark square
with one matching set of four tan triangles.

4 With right sides facing up, place one triangle on
one corner of a dark square, aligning the straight
edges. Apply a dab of glue to each point of the triangle
to secure it. Sew ⅛" from the diagonal edge of the
triangle. Repeat to appliqué a triangle on each corner
of the block. Make 11 Square in a Square blocks.

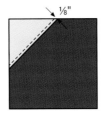

Topstitch.

Make 11 blocks,
4½" × 4½".

Assembling the Table Runner

Press the seam allowances as indicated by the arrows.

1 Lay out three rows of seven blocks, alternating the Four Petal and Square-in-a-Square blocks as shown. Join the blocks in each row, and then join the rows. The runner center should measure 12½" × 28½".

Table-runner assembly

Charmed, I'm Sure!

from **LYNNE HAGMEIER**

Lynne Hagmeier has miles of Midwestern charm, known to quilters as Kansas Troubles Quilters (KTQuilts.com).

- **What charms me most about charm packs is** that there's a wonderful little piece of each fabric from the collection in every charm pack.

- **Same or different? If you're making a project with multiple charm packs, are you more likely to use two or three from the same collection or from different collections?** Different.

- **About those pinked edges, here's my advice for taking them into account when you sew:** Measure your precut to see where the 5" dimension is, and adjust your seam allowance accordingly.

- **Besides a 5" charm-square, my other go-to precut shape is** a 10" Layer Cake square.

- **If I taught at Quilters' Finishing School, I'd teach the students to** perfect their technique for continuous binding. A flat, even binding is the perfect finish to a charming quilt.

- **If I had to pick a "lucky" charm out of a charm pack, I'd choose** a tan background with a multicolored small print—the perfect background!

- **In Charm School, you learn the social graces. But in Quilter's Charm School you learn that** all charms play nicely together—the more different prints and fabric lines, the better.

2 Sew the 2½" × 28½" black strips to the long sides of the runner center; press the seam allowances toward the borders. Sew the 2½" × 16½" black strips to the short sides of the runner; press. The runner top should measure 16½" × 32½".

Finishing the Table Runner

Go to ShopMartingale.com/HowtoQuilt for more details on quilting and finishing.

1 Layer the backing, batting, and runner top; baste the layers together. Hand or machine quilt as desired. The runner shown was machine quilted in a square grid, and the petals were outlined and echo quilted to highlight the design.

2 Use the black 2½" × 42" strips to make the binding and attach it to the runner.

3 Hand stitch a button at the center of each Four Petal block.

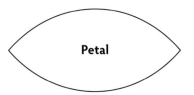

Petal

Hexagon Braid *by Jenny Doan*

- FINISHED TABLE RUNNER: 24" × 52"
- FINISHED BRAID: 5¾" × 41½"
- CHARM PACKS NEEDED: ■ □ □

Create a complex braided look with patchwork by using a half-hexagon shape in an easy repeated-stacking process. The hexagon pattern is designed to fit perfectly on a charm square, so cutting is a breeze.

Materials

Yardage is based on 42"-wide fabric. Charm squares are 5" × 5".

1 charm pack (40 squares) of assorted bright prints for braids

⅓ yard of white solid for sashing and inner border

½ yard of pink print for outer border

⅓ yard of gray print for binding

1¾ yards of fabric for backing (with vertical seam)

29" × 56" piece of batting

Cutting

All measurements include ¼"-wide seam allowances.

From the charm squares, cut:

80 rectangles, 2½" × 5"; from each rectangle, cut
1 half hexagon using the template on page 29

From the white solid, cut:

4 strips, 2½" × 42"; crosscut 1 of the strips into 2
pieces, 2½" × 18"

From the pink print, cut:

4 strips, 3½" × 42"

From the gray print, cut:

4 strips, 2½" × 42"

Assembling the Braid

Press the seam allowances as indicated by the arrows.

1 Organize the hexagons into two stacks of 42. Place
two half hexagons from one pile right side up,
aligning one edge as shown. Flip the bottom hexagon
to the wrong side, placing it right sides together with
the top hexagon. Match the bottom edges, making
sure a dog-ear extends by exactly ¼" at the corner.
Sew the bottom edges.

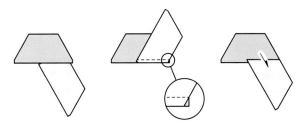

2 Sew the next hexagon to the unit with the long
edge of the new hexagon adjoining the edge with
the seam that was just sewn. Continue adding the
remaining hexagons from the pile in this manner.

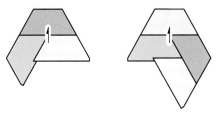

3 Make two braids of 40 hexagons each. Trim each
braid as shown to measure 6¼" × 42".

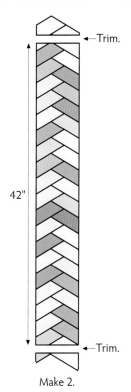

Make 2.

Charmed, I'm Sure!

from **JENNY DOAN**

Jenny Doan (MissouriQuiltCo.com) has never met a charm pack she didn't like.

- **What charms me most about charm packs is** convenience! I know if I want to make a baby quilt, I need one charm pack, two packs will make a crib quilt, three make a lap, and four will make a twin-size. Convenience!

- **Same or different? If you're making a project with multiple charm packs, are you more likely to use two or three from the same collection or from different collections?** Same.

- **This works like a charm for me every time:** Press from the top and then flip the fabric over and, when possible, press the seam allowances to the darker fabric.

- **About those pinked edges, here's my advice for taking them into account when you sew:** The pinked edge does crazy things to our perfect quarter-inch, so for me a consistent seam allowance is more important than a perfect quarter-inch. It's a personal preference, but I like to see those points sticking out under the edge of the presser foot.

- **Besides a 5" charm square, my other go-to precut shape is** a 2½" strip.

- **If I taught at Quilters' Finishing School, I'd teach the students to** go at their own pace. Enjoy the journey.

- **If I had to pick a "lucky" charm out of a charm pack, I'd choose** one that had lots of colors in it so it would bring all the other squares together.

- **In Charm School, you learn the social graces. But in Quilter's Charm School you learn that** finished is better than perfect. Sewing is a practiced skill and the more you sew the better you will get.

Assembling the Table Runner

Press the seam allowances as indicated by the arrows.

1 Sew one white 2½" × 42" strip between the two braids. The runner center should measure 14" × 42".

2 For the inner border, sew one white 2½" × 42" strip to each side of the runner center. Sew the 2½" × 18" white strips to the top and bottom of the runner. The runner should measure 18" × 46".

3 Cut one of the pink strips into two pieces, 3½" × 18", and sew them to the top and bottom of the runner. Join the remaining three pink strips end to end, and from this long strip, cut two side border strips to fit the length of the runner (which should be 52" long). Sew these strips to the sides of the runner. Press. The runner should measure 24" × 52".

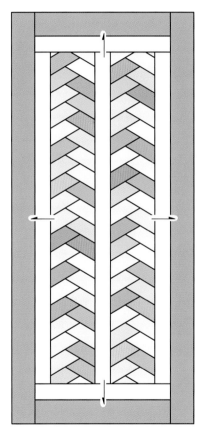

Table-runner assembly

Finishing the Table Runner

Go to ShopMartingale.com/HowtoQuilt for more details on quilting and finishing.

1 Layer the backing, batting, and runner top; baste the layers together. Hand or machine quilt as desired. The runner shown was machine quilted in an allover flower and swirl pattern.

2 Use the gray print 2½"-wide strips to make the binding and attach it to the runner.

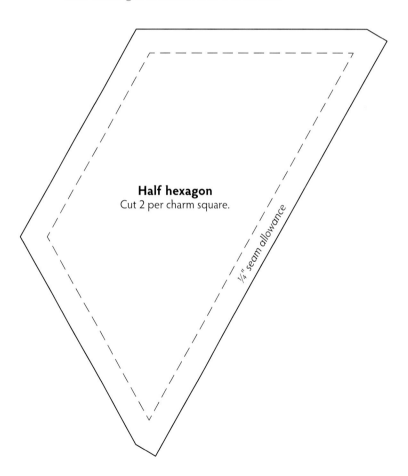

Half hexagon
Cut 2 per charm square.

¼" seam allowance

Two-Pack Buzz by Barbara Groves and Mary Jacobson

- **FINISHED QUILT: 42½" × 50½"**
- **FINISHED BLOCK: 8" × 8"**
- **CHARM PACKS NEEDED: ■ ■ □**

Combine two charm packs of cheerful prints to make these fun Buzz Saw blocks. Use two identical charm packs or mix two different packs with coordinating colors for a more varied effect.

Materials

Yardage is based on 42"-wide fabric. Charm squares are 5" × 5".

2 charm packs of assorted bright prints for blocks (you'll need 78 squares)

1⅝ yards of white solid for blocks, inner border, and outer border

½ yard of aqua print for binding

2¾ yards of fabric for backing

49" × 57" piece of batting

Cutting

All measurements include ¼"-wide seam allowances. Note that you'll cut 38 charm squares into rectangles and reserve 40 for making the half-square-triangle units.

From *each* of 38 charm squares, cut:

3 rectangles, 1½" × 4½" (114 total)

From the white solid, cut:

5 strips, 5" × 42"; crosscut the strips into 40 squares, 5" × 5"

5 strips, 3½" × 42"

5 strips, 1½" × 42"; crosscut 1 strip into:

    4 rectangles, 1½" × 3½"

    4 rectangles, 1½" × 2½"

From the aqua print, cut:

5 strips, 2½" × 42"

Assembling the Blocks

Press the seam allowances as indicated by the arrows.

1 Draw a diagonal line from corner to corner on the wrong side of the white squares. Place one print square and one white square right sides together with the white square on top. Sew ¼" from each side of the drawn line. Cut along the line to yield two half-square-triangle units. Referring to "Trim and Stack" at right, trim the units to measure 4½" square. Make 80.

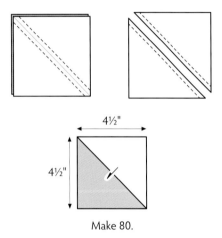

Make 80.

2 Crosscut each unit into three 1½" × 4½" segments as shown. Keep the matching sets of segments together.

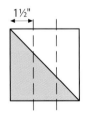 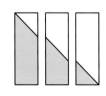

TRIM AND STACK

After trimming the half-square-triangle units, stack them with the print triangle at bottom left. Aligning the stack will help you keep the units organized and prevent you from slicing one in the wrong direction.

3 Rearrange three matching segments as shown. Select one 1½" × 4½" rectangle of a different print. Join the three segments and the print rectangle. Make 80 pieced units that measure 4½" square.

Make 80.

4 Lay out two rows of two units, orienting the segments as shown. Join the units in each vertical row, and then join the rows. Make 20 blocks that measure 8½" square.

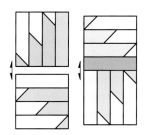 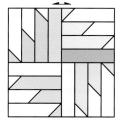

Make 20 blocks,
8½" × 8½".

Assembling the Pieced Borders

Press the seam allowances as indicated by the arrows.

1 Lay out nine 1½" × 4½" rectangles and two white 1½" × 3½" rectangles end to end as shown. Join the rectangles. The border should measure 1½" × 42½". Make two.

Make 2 borders, 1½" × 42½".

2 Lay out eight print 1½" × 4½" rectangles and two white 1½" × 2½" rectangles end to end as shown. Join the rectangles. The border should measure 1½" × 36½". Make two.

Make 2 borders, 1½" × 36½".

Assembling the Quilt Top

Press the seam allowances as indicated by the arrows.

1 Lay out the blocks in five rows of four as shown in the quilt assembly diagram. Join the blocks in each row, and then join the rows. The quilt center should measure 32½" × 40½".

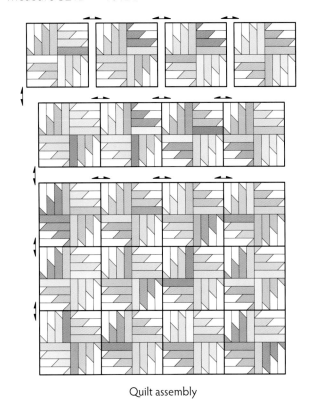

Quilt assembly

2 Trim two of the white 1½" × 42" strips to 40½" long. Sew the strips to the sides of the quilt center. Trim the two remaining white 1½" × 42" strips to measure 1½" × 34½". Sew these strips to the top and bottom of the quilt center. The quilt should measure 34½" × 42½".

3 Sew the pieced 1½" × 42½" borders to the sides of the quilt, and then sew the pieced 1½" × 36½" borders to the top and bottom of the quilt. The quilt should measure 36½" × 44½".

4 Join the white 3½" × 42" strips end to end. From this strip, cut two strips, 3½" × 44½", and sew them to the sides of the quilt. Cut two strips, 3½" × 42½", and sew them to the top and bottom of the quilt. The quilt should measure 42½" × 50½".

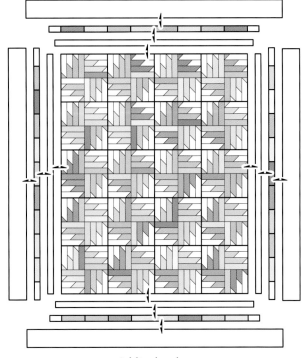

Adding borders

Finishing the Quilt

For more details on quilting and finishing, you can visit ShopMartingale.com/HowtoQuilt.

1 Layer the backing, batting, and quilt top; baste the layers together.

2 Hand or machine quilt as desired. The quilt shown was machine quilted with a flower design in the center of the blocks and an allover loop design in the background. The borders are quilted with a vine and loop design.

3 Use the aqua 2½"-wide strips to make the binding and attach it to the quilt.

Charmed, I'm Sure!

from **BARBARA GROVES** and **MARY JACOBSON**

Barbara Groves and Mary Jacobson are charmed and charmed alike, considering this sister/sister act is the duo known as Me and My Sister Designs (MeandMySisterDesigns.com).

- **What charms us most about charm packs is** the size. We love getting at least one of everything from a fabric collection in an affordable bundle.

- **Same or different? If you're making a project with multiple charm packs, are you more likely to use two or three from the same collection or from different collections?** Same!

- **This works like a charm for us every time:** Whenever I make a mistake and something needs to be unsewn, I show it to my sister, the perfectionist. All I have to say is, "I'm going to leave it," and she can't stand it . . . so she rips it out for me. (Names have been redacted to protect the innocent.)

- **About those pinked edges, here's our advice for taking them into account when you sew:** Mary: They drive me crazy. I want to trim them all off. Barb: I just make sure to measure and sew from the very outer pinked edge.

- **Besides a 5" charm square, our other go-to precut shape is** a fat quarter. (BUT, we really LOVE six-yard chunks!)

- **If we taught at Quilters' Finishing School, we'd teach the students to** hand sew their binding. It's so relaxing!

- **If we had to pick a "lucky" charm out of a charm pack, we'd choose** one that is lime green. It goes with everything!

- **In Charm School, you learn the social graces. But in Quilter's Charm School you learn that** it's okay if your points don't always match, as long as you're having fun—and then ask your machine quilter to stitch over those spots whenever possible.

Scrappy Christmas by Anne Sutton

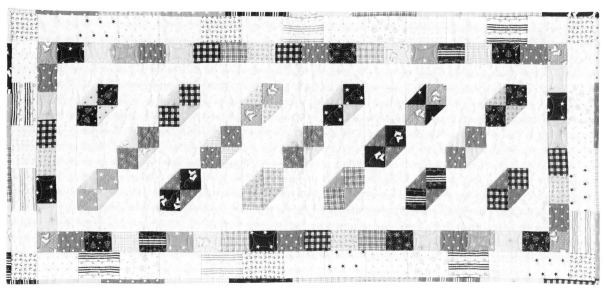

- **FINISHED TABLE RUNNER: 19½" × 43½"**
- **FINISHED BLOCK: 3" × 3"**
- **CHARM PACKS NEEDED:** ■ ■ ◻

Use two charm packs in festive red, pink, green, and brown prints to make a cute yuletide table runner. The small-scale Hourglass blocks are reminiscent of tasty Christmas candy.

Materials

Yardage is based on 42"-wide fabric. Charm squares are 5" × 5".

2 charm packs of assorted red, green, cream, tan, and brown prints for rows, borders, and binding. You'll need 43 assorted medium/dark (collectively referred to as "dark") and 19 light squares.

⅝ yard of cream print for background

1½ yards of fabric for backing

25" × 49" piece of batting

Cutting

From the dark charm squares, cut:

17 squares, 2½" × 2½"
48 rectangles, 2" × 2½"
17 matching pairs of squares, 2" × 2" (34 total)
1 matching set of 4 squares, 2" × 2"
31 rectangles, 2¼" × 5", for binding

From the light charm squares, cut:

36 rectangles, 2½" × 3½"
1 matching set of 4 squares, 2½" × 2½"

From the cream print for background, cut:

2 strips, 3½" × 42"; crosscut the strips into 16 squares, 3½" × 3½"
2 strips, 2½" × 42"; crosscut the strips into 17 squares, 2½" × 2½"
3 strips, 2" × 42"; crosscut the strips into:
    2 strips, 2" × 33½"
    2 strips, 2" × 12½"

Assembling the Rows

Press the seam allowances as indicated by the arrows.

1 Draw a diagonal line from corner to corner on the wrong side of each 2½" cream square. Place each marked square right sides together with one dark 2½" square, with the marked square on top. Sew ¼" from each side of the drawn line. Cut along the line to yield two half-square-triangle units. Trim each unit to measure 2" square. Make 34.

Make 34.

2 Lay out two matching half-square-triangle units and two matching dark 2" squares in two rows of two as shown. Join the units in each row, and then join the rows to make an hourglass unit. The unit should measure 3½" square. Make 17.

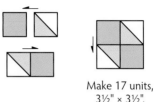

Make 17 units,
3½" × 3½".

3 Sew one cream 3½" square between two hourglass units. The row should measure 3½" × 9½". Make 6.

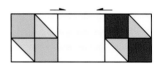

Make 6 units,
3½" × 9½".

4 Sew one hourglass unit between two cream 3½" squares. The row should measure 3½" × 9½". Make 5.

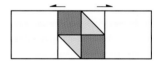

Make 5 units,
3½" × 9½".

Assembling the Borders and Binding

Press the seam allowances as indicated by the arrows.

1 For the middle border, sew 18 dark 2" × 2½" rectangles end to end. The strip should measure 2" × 36½". Make two. Sew six dark 2" × 2½" rectangles end to end, and then sew two of the four matching dark 2" squares to the ends of the strip. The strip should measure 2" × 15½". Make two.

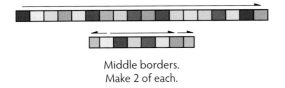

Middle borders.
Make 2 of each.

2 For the outer border, join 13 light 2½" × 3½" rectangles end to end. The strip should measure 2½" × 39½". Make two. Join five light 2½" × 3½" rectangles end to end, and then sew two light 2½" squares to the ends of the strip. The strip should measure 2½" × 19½". Make two.

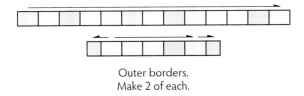

Outer borders.
Make 2 of each.

3 Join the dark 2¼" × 5" binding rectangles end to end to make the pieced binding. Press the seam allowances open to reduce bulk.

Assembling the Table Runner

Press the seam allowances as indicated by the arrows.

1 Lay out the block rows, alternating them as shown in the runner assembly diagram below. Join the rows. The runner should measure 9½" × 33½".

2 Sew the cream 2" × 33½" strips to the sides of the runner center. Sew the cream 2" × 12½" strips to the top and bottom of the runner center. Sew the middle border strips and outer border strips to the runner. The runner should measure 19½" × 43½".

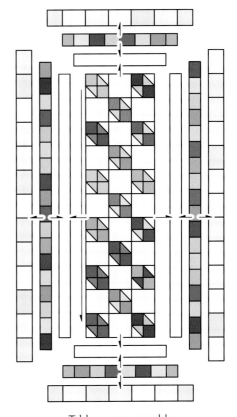

Table-runner assembly

Charmed, I'm Sure!

from ANNE SUTTON

Add two parts charm and one part sweetness to equal the engaging personality of designer Anne Sutton of Bunny Hill Designs (BunnyHillDesigns.com).

- **What charms me most about charm packs is this:** Who doesn't like a 5" sample of every fabric in the line?

- **Same or different? If you're making a project with multiple charm packs, are you more likely to use two or three from the same collection or from different collections?** Same.

- **This works like a charm for me every time:** Starch away! I use Faultless Premium Starch (hint: look for the gold lid).

- **About those pinked edges, here's my advice for taking them into account when you sew:** Ignore them and sew with a ¼" seam allowance.

- **Besides a 5" charm-square, my other go-to precut shape is** a fat-quarter bundle.

- **If I taught at Quilters' Finishing School, I'd teach the students to** finish the ends of the binding professionally—smooth with no lumps or bumps!

- **If I had to pick a "lucky" charm out of a charm pack, I'd choose** one with a small print that I could fussy-cut.

- **In Charm School, you learn the social graces. But in Quilter's Charm School you learn that** one of the charms in a charm pack is always going to stand out from the others. Be sure and use it in your quilt. It will add interest.

Finishing the Table Runner

For more details on quilting and finishing, you can visit ShopMartingale.com/HowtoQuilt.

1 Layer the backing, batting, and table-runner top; baste the layers together. Hand or machine quilt as desired. The runner shown was machine quilted with a snowflake design in the background and quilted in the ditch around the blocks and borders. The inner border rectangles were framed with an orange peel design. The outer border squares were quilted with a loop design evocative of a Christmas tree.

2 Use the pieced 2¼"-wide strip to make the binding and attach it to the runner.

Sweet Stripes by Karla Eisenach

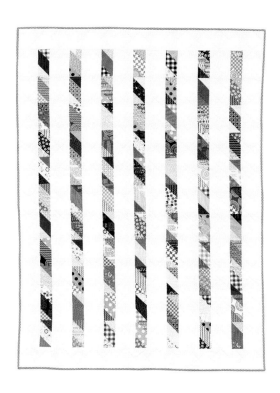

- **FINISHED QUILT:** 42½" × 57"
- **FINISHED BLOCK:** 2" × 4½"
- **CHARM PACKS NEEDED:** ■ ■ □

Stitch an eye-catching striped quilt from two charm packs in the timeless color combination of black, red, and cream. The vertical rows are fast and fun to piece, so the quilt top comes together in a flash.

Materials

Yardage is based on 42"-wide fabric. Charm squares are 5" × 5".

2 charm packs of assorted red, black, cream, and gray prints for patchwork rows (you'll need 77 squares)
1½ yards of cream gingham for background and border
½ yard of red-and-white stripe for binding
2¾ yards of fabric for backing
49" × 64" piece of batting

Cutting

All measurements include ¼"-wide seam allowances.

From *each* charm square, cut:
1 rectangle, 2½" × 5" (77 total)
2 squares, 2½" × 2½" (154 total)

From the *lengthwise* grain of the cream gingham, cut:
8 strips, 4" × 50"
2 strips, 4" × 42½"

From the red-and-white stripe, cut:
5 strips, 2½" × 42"

Assembling the Pieced Rows

Press the seam allowances as indicated by the arrows.

1 Select two squares and one rectangle, all with different prints. Draw a diagonal line from corner to corner on the wrong side of the print 2½" squares. Place the marked squares right sides together with the rectangle, orienting the drawn lines as shown. Sew along the marked lines. Trim the unit ¼" outside of each sewn line; press. Repeat to make 77 units.

 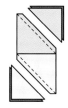 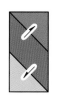

Make 77 units,
2½" × 5½".

2 Join 11 units end to end to make one pieced row measuring 2½" × 50". Make 7 rows.

Make 7 rows, 2½" × 50".

LIKE A CHARM

"For quilts with many seam intersections, I press seam allowances open, which makes matching intersections easy." ~Karla

Charmed, I'm Sure!

from **KARLA EISENACH**

Karla Eisenach is both sweet and charming, as one third of the design trio that is Sweetwater (TheSweetwaterCo.com).

■ **What charms me most about charm packs** is that you get an assortment of colors and prints that are meant to be together.

■ **Same or different? If you're making a project with multiple charm packs, are you more likely to use two or three from the same collection or from different collections?** Different.

■ **About those pinked edges, here's my advice for taking them into account when you sew:** Don't stress about them. As long as you're consistent with your seam allowance, you will be okay.

■ **Besides a 5" charm-square, my other go-to precut shape is** a 2½" square.

■ **If I taught at Quilters' Finishing School, I'd teach the students to** think of binding as the frame on their piece of art—their finished quilt.

■ **If I had to pick a "lucky" charm out of a charm pack, I'd choose** one that is a little bit bold—a show-off.

Assembling the Quilt Top

Press the seam allowances as indicated by the arrows. Lay out the pieced rows and gingham 4" × 50" strips, alternating them as shown in the quilt assembly diagram. Join the rows and strips. The quilt should measure 42½" × 50". Sew the gingham 4" × 42½" strips to the top and bottom of the quilt.

Finishing the Quilt

Go to ShopMartingale.com/HowtoQuilt for more details on quilting and finishing.

1 Layer the backing, batting, and quilt top; baste the layers together. Hand or machine quilt as desired. The quilt shown was machine quilted with a diamond pattern in the borders and sashing.

2 Use the red and white 2½"-wide strips to make the binding and attach it to the quilt.

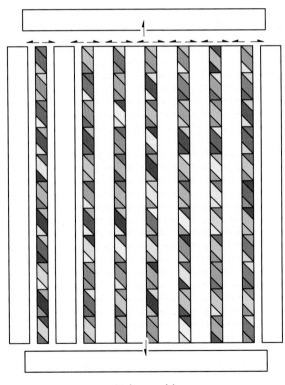

Quilt assembly

Heading West by Pat Sloan

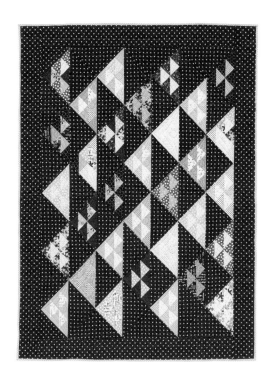

- **FINISHED QUILT:** 45½" × 61"
- **FINISHED BLOCK:** 7⅜" × 7⅜"
- **CHARM PACKS NEEDED:** ■ ■ □

All blocks point west in Pat's playful triangle-themed quilt. Combine two charm packs of scrappy green, blue, and red prints with a fun and simple polka dot background.

Materials

Yardage is based on 42"-wide fabric. Charm squares are 5" × 5".

2 charm packs of assorted green, navy, red, aqua, gray, and white prints for blocks. You'll need at least 48 medium/dark (collectively referred to as "dark") and 24 light squares.

2½ yards of charcoal polka dot cotton/linen blend for blocks, setting triangles, and border

½ yard of green print for binding

3 yards of fabric for backing

51" × 68" piece of batting

COLOR COMBOS

Pat used the same two colors and prints in the pieced section of most blocks. To get the best use out of the charm packs, she also made scrappy blocks. Depending on the assortment in your charm pack, you can mix or match fabrics.

Cutting

All measurements include ¼"-wide seam allowances.

For *each of 24* dark charm squares:

Trim to 4¾" square first; then cut into quarters
diagonally to yield 4 triangles (96 total)

From the charcoal polka dot, cut *from the lengthwise grain:*

1 strip, 22" × 64"; crosscut the strip into:
    2 strips, 5" × 64"
    2 strips, 5" × 54"

From the remaining charcoal polka dot, cut:

3 strips, 8½" × 42"; crosscut into 14 squares,
    8½" × 8½". Cut each square in half diagonally to
    yield 2 block triangles (28 total, 1 is extra).
3 squares, 11½" × 11½"; cut each square into quarters
    diagonally to yield 4 setting triangles (12 total; 2
    are extra)
1 square, 6½" × 6½"; cut the square in half diagonally
    to yield 2 corner triangles

From the green print for binding, cut:

5 strips, 2½" × 42"

Assembling the Blocks

Press the seam allowances as indicated by the arrows.
The quilt contains 27 blocks and five half blocks. Each
block contains three half-square-triangle units, three
dark triangles, and one charcoal 8½" triangle. Each half
block is composed of the pieced triangle unit only.

1 Select 24 dark and 24 light charm squares. Draw
diagonal lines from corner to corner in both
directions on the wrong side of each light square.

2 Place a marked light square right sides together
with a dark square. Sew a *scant* ¼" inside the
perimeter of the squares. Cut along the lines to yield
four half-square-triangle units; press carefully. Trim the
units to measure 3" square. Make 96.

Make 24.

Make 96 units,
3" × 3".

HANDLE WITH CARE

*Note that the outer edges of the
half-square-triangle units are cut
on the bias, which is less stable
than the lengthwise and crosswise
fabric grains. Be very careful not
to stretch the edges of the units as
you press them. Pat uses spray
starch to add stability.*

Charmed, I'm Sure!

from **PAT SLOAN**

Pat Sloan (PatSloan.com) is at her most charming when she's teaching others to quilt!

- **What charms me most about charm packs is that** I love having a piece of the full range of fabrics in a line. It helps me with my fabric choices!

- **Same or different? If you're making a project with multiple charm packs, are you more likely to use two or three of the same collection or from different collections?** Same.

- **This works like a charm for me every time:** Using the half-square triangle reference chart in my *Teach Me To Sew Triangles* book.

- **About those pinked edges, here's my advice for taking them into account when you sew:** I consider them part of my charm and measure from the outside point. They don't bother me at all.

- **Besides a 5" charm-square, my other go-to precut shape is** a nice, big, Layer Cake square. Because it's 10", I can do so much with it!

- **If I had to pick a "lucky" charm out of a charm pack, I'd choose** one that has dots. I'm CRAZY for dots! It's delightful to find a beautiful, yummy dot in my charm pack.

- **In Charm School, you learn the social graces. But in Quilter's Charm School you learn** that your charm pack is an amazing design unit that, when paired with a blender, will make 84 half-square triangles. In turn, those can turn into a zillion different quilt designs!

3 Choose a color/print combination for the pieced half of each block (see "Color Combos" on page 45). Lay out three half-square-triangle units and three small triangles as shown. Join the pieces in two sections; join the sections. Make 32 pieced triangles.

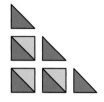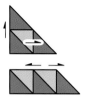

Make 32.

4 Select 27 pieced triangles for the blocks and reserve five units for the half blocks. Sew a charcoal 8½" triangle to each of the 27 units as shown, using a scant ¼" seam allowance. Square up each block to measure 7⅞" square.

Make 27 blocks,
7⅞" × 7⅞".

Assembling the Quilt Top

Press the seam allowances as indicated by the arrows.

1 Lay out the blocks in seven diagonal rows, placing them on point as shown in the quilt assembly diagram. Place the setting triangles along the top, bottom, and left sides, filling in the spaces between the blocks. Place the corner triangles in the left top

and bottom corners. Place the half blocks along the right side. Join the pieces in each diagonal row, and then join the rows. The quilt should measure approximately 36½" × 52".

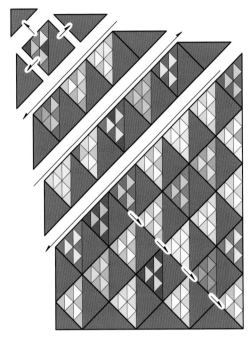

Quilt assembly

2 Measure the quilt top horizontally through the center. Trim the short 5"-wide strips to the measurement, and then sew them to the top and bottom of the quilt. Press the seam allowances toward the borders. Measure the quilt top vertically through the center, including the borders, and then trim and sew the long 5"-wide strips to the sides of the quilt top; press. The quilt should measure 45½" × 61".

Finishing the Quilt

Go to ShopMartingale.com/HowtoQuilt for more details on quilting and finishing.

1 Layer the backing, batting, and quilt top; baste the layers together. Hand or machine quilt as desired. The quilt shown was machine quilted with rows of circles in the borders and an echoing curved triangle design in the blocks.

2 Use the green 2½"-wide strips to make the binding and attach it to the quilt. Pat used a machine sewing method to attach her double-fold binding. She first sewed it to the back of the quilt with the raw edges aligned. She then folded the binding to the front and blanket stitched along the fold from the front of the quilt.

A CHARMING FINISH

"If I taught at Quilters' Finishing School, I'd teach the students to make triangle labels for all their quilts. Fold a square in half diagonally. The two raw-edge sides are sewn into your binding with only one side left to hand stitch!" ~Pat

Prairie Nights by Kathy Schmitz

- **FINISHED QUILT:** 50" × 50"
- **FINISHED BLOCK:** 10½ × 10½"
- **CHARM PACKS NEEDED:** ■■□

A combination of red, black, and tan prints and striking Hourglass blocks makes for a simple yet dramatic design. This throw-sized quilt is perfect for cozying up on a chilly autumn evening.

Materials

Yardage is based on 42"-wide fabric. Charm squares are 5" × 5".

2 charm packs of assorted red, black, and tan prints for blocks and sashing (you'll need 18 red, 18 black, and 40 tan squares)
2⅛ yards of black print for blocks, borders, sashing, and binding
3¼ yards of fabric for backing
56" × 56" piece of batting

Cutting

All measurements include ¼"-wide seam allowances.

From 4 of the tan charm squares, cut:
4 squares, 2½" × 2½" (16 total)

From the black print, cut:
2 strips, 11" × 42"; crosscut the strips into 24 strips, 2½" × 11"
5 strips, 5½" × 42"; crosscut 1 of the strips into 2 rectangles, 5½" × 10"
1 strip, 4" × 42"; crosscut the strip into 9 squares, 4" × 4"
5 strips, 2½" × 42"

Assembling the Blocks

Press the seam allowances as indicated by the arrows.

1 Draw a diagonal line from corner to corner on the wrong side of 36 tan charm squares. Pair one tan charm square with one black charm square, right sides together and with the tan square on top. Sew ¼" from both sides of the drawn line. Cut along the drawn line, and then cut perpendicular to the line to yield four pieces; press.

2 Place two pieces right sides together, matching the seams and opposite colors. Sew the long edge. Press and trim the hourglass unit to measure 4" square. Make 36 black and 36 red hourglass units.

Make 36 of each,
4" × 4".

3 Arrange four black hourglass units, four red hourglass units, and one black 4" square in three rows of three as shown. Join the units, and then join

the rows. Make nine blocks measuring 11" square, including the seam allowances.

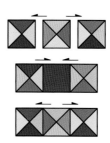 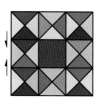

Make 9 blocks,
11" × 11".

Assembling the Quilt

Press the seam allowances as indicated by the arrows.

1 Lay out three rows of blocks and black 2½" × 11" strips alternating with three rows of black strips and tan 2½" squares as shown in the quilt assembly diagram. Join the units in each row, and then join the rows. The quilt center should measure 40" square.

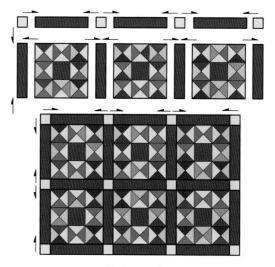

Quilt assembly

2 Trim two of the black 5½" × 42" strips to the width of the quilt, which should be 40", and sew them to the top and bottom of the quilt. Press the seam allowances toward the strips. The quilt should measure approximately 40" × 50".

3 Sew a black 5½" × 10" rectangle to one end of each remaining 5½" × 42" strip. Press the seam allowances open. Measure the quilt vertically through the center; it should be 50" long. Trim the two pieced strips to this measurement and sew them to the sides of the quilt; press.

Finishing the Quilt

For more details on quilting and finishing, you can visit ShopMartingale.com/HowtoQuilt.

1 Layer the backing, batting, and quilt top; baste the layers together. Hand or machine quilt as desired. The quilt shown was machine quilted with an allover swirl and vine design using tan thread for contrast.

2 Use the black 2½"-wide strips to make the binding and attach it to the quilt.

Charmed, I'm Sure!

from **KATHY SCHMITZ**

Kathy Schmitz (KathySchmitz.com) can charm the paint off a paintbrush! That's the secret to how she designs such spectacular prints for her Moda fabric lines.

■ **What charms me most about charm packs is** that I hope their charm will rub off on me. I am a bit of a klutz.

■ **Same or different? If you're making a project with multiple charm packs, are you more likely to use two or three of the same collection or from different collections?** Same.

■ **This works like a charm for me every time:** Asking my mom to come and help me. This works best if I supply her with desserts.

■ **About those pinked edges, here's my advice for taking them into account when you sew:** Was I supposed to pay attention to them? I guess if I really think about it, I measure from the outside points. Or, ask my mom for help again. Okay, okay, you got me. I just like having my mom around!

■ **Besides a 5" charm-square, my other go-to precut shape is** a Layer Cake 10" square. Just the name makes me smile!

■ **If I taught at Quilters' Finishing School, I'd teach the students** to hand quilt (if it's not a huge quilt). I love that look!

■ **If I had to pick a "lucky" charm out of a charm pack, I'd choose** one that has tiny dots on it! I love little dots.

■ **In Charm School, you learn the social graces. But in Quilter's Charm School you learn** it's okay to be left out. Those little squares that don't have a home in a project are just the right size for making pincushions. You can NEVER have enough pincushions.

Spring Mosaic by Sandy Gervais

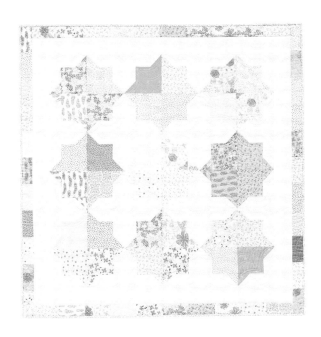

- FINISHED QUILT: 49½" × 49½"
- FINISHED BLOCK: 13½" × 13½"
- CHARM PACKS NEEDED: ■■☐

Soft shades of yellow, orange, and green are ideal for a quilt that will bring a touch of nature indoors. Construct the quick blocks from charm squares and folded-corner units, and get the most out of the charm packs by using the remaining squares for a coordinating pieced border.

Materials

Yardage is based on 42"-wide fabric. Charm squares are 5" × 5".

2 matching charm packs (75 charms total) of assorted green, aqua, orange, cream, tan, and yellow prints for blocks and outer border (see "Matchmaking" below)

1½ yards of cream solid for background and inner border

½ yard of cream print for binding

3¼ yards of fabric for backing

56" × 56" piece of batting

MATCHMAKING

Each block quadrant requires four coordinating squares from one charm pack and four identical squares from the second pack. Your charm pack might not have enough of one color or print for nine full sets of eight squares. If so, instead choose eight assorted charm squares for each block.

Cutting

All measurements include ¼"-wide seam allowances. The quilt has nine blocks that require eight charm squares each.

CUTTING THE CHARM SQUARES

Select and organize the eight charm squares for each block before cutting (refer to "Matchmaking" on page 55). For each block, designate one set of four squares for the four-patch unit and one set of four squares for the folded-corner units.

From *each* of the 36 charm squares in the folded-corner sets, cut:

1 rectangle, 2½" × 5" (36 total; reserve for the outer border)

2 squares, 2½" × 2½" (72 total)

From the remaining charm squares, cut:

6 rectangles, 2½" × 5"

CUTTING THE BORDERS AND BINDING

From the cream solid, cut:

3 strips, 7" × 42"; crosscut the strips into 36 rectangles, 2½" × 7"

5 strips, 3½" × 42"

5 strips, 2½" × 42"; crosscut the strips into 36 rectangles, 2½" × 5"

From the cream print for binding, cut:

6 strips, 2½" × 42"

Assembling the Blocks

Press the seam allowances as indicated by the arrows.

1 Lay out four charm squares for one block in two rows of two. Join the squares in each row, and then join the rows to make a four-patch unit measuring 9½" square.

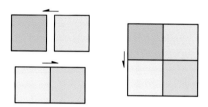

2 Draw a diagonal line from corner to corner on the wrong side of the 2½" squares that match the top-left square in the four-patch unit. Place one marked square on the end of a cream 2½" × 5" rectangle with right sides together. Sew along the line. Trim *only* the square fabric ¼" from the line, and then press. Repeat with the remaining matching square and a 2½" × 7" cream rectangle. Repeat to make a pair of matching folded-corner units for the bottom-right square in the four-patch unit.

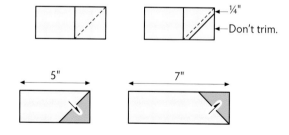

3 Repeat the process from step 2 with the four remaining 2½" squares to make two additional pairs of matching 5"- and 7"-long folded-corner units, but orient the marked line in the opposite direction from the units in step 2. These units will match the top-right and bottom-left squares.

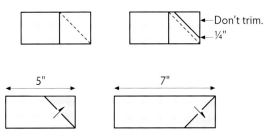

←Don't trim.
←¼"

4 Lay out the folded-corner units around the edges of the four-patch unit, matching the placement of the prints as shown.

5 Join the folded-corner units in pairs as shown. Sew the top and bottom units to the four-patch unit, and then sew the side units. Repeat with each set of matching pieces to make nine blocks measuring 13½" square.

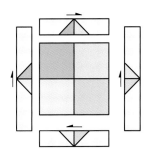
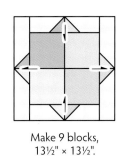

Make 9 blocks,
13½" × 13½".

Assembling the Quilt

Press the seam allowances as indicated by the arrows.

1 Lay out three rows of three blocks. Join the blocks in each row, and then join the rows. The quilt center should measure 39½" square.

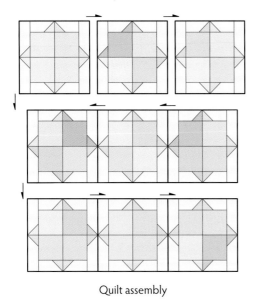

Quilt assembly

2 Trim two of the cream 3½" × 42" strips to measure 39½", and then sew them to the top and bottom of the quilt center; press. The quilt should measure 39½" × 45½". Join the remaining 3½" × 42" strips end to end. From this long strip, cut two strips measuring 45½" long. Sew the strips to the sides of the quilt; press. The quilt should measure 45½" square.

3 Join 10 assorted 2½" × 5" rectangles end to end; press the seam allowances in one direction. The border should measure 2½" × 45½". Repeat to make a second border from 10 rectangles. Sew the borders to the top and bottom of the quilt. The quilt should measure 45½" × 49½". Join 11 assorted 2½" × 5" rectangles end to end; press. Repeat to make a second border from the remaining rectangles. Trim these borders to measure 49½" long. Sew the borders to the sides of the quilt; press.

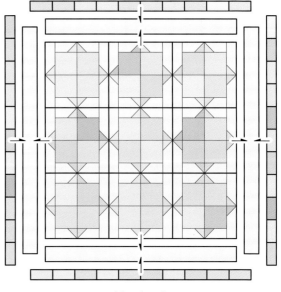

Adding borders

Finishing the Quilt

Go to ShopMartingale.com/
HowtoQuilt for more details on
quilting and finishing.

1 Layer the backing, batting, and
quilt top; baste the layers
together. Hand or machine quilt as
desired. The quilt shown was
machine quilted with an echoing
curved design in the center of
each block. The cream background
is quilted with a curved cross
design, and the outer border has a
simple scalloped design.

2 Use the cream 2½"-wide
strips to make the binding
and attach it to the quilt.

Charmed, I'm Sure!

from **SANDY GERVAIS**

Sandy Gervais (PiecesfromMyHeart.net) is one of Moda Fabrics'
original lucky charms. She's been a fabric designer with Moda for
more than 22 years.

■ **What charms me most about charm packs is that** I have always
loved any kind of puzzle. I do the Word Jumble and Suduko puzzles in
the paper every day. I think of making a charm pack quilt as a bit of a
puzzle. What can I make with these squares? How will I make three red
squares work, when I really need four? I like the challenge.

■ **Same or different? If you're making a project with multiple charm
packs, are you more likely to use two or three of the same collection
or from different collections?** Same.

■ **This works like a charm for me every time:** Pin and press. I need both.

■ **About those pinked edges, here's my advice for taking them into
account when you sew:** Use the outside pinked tips as if they were the
cut line. Never trim them off!

■ **Besides a 5" charm square, my other go-to precut shape is** a Layer
Cake 10" square.

■ **If I taught at Quilters' Finishing School, I'd teach the students that**
getting it done is more important than perfection.

■ **If I had to pick a "lucky" charm out of a charm pack, I'd choose**
whichever one makes the quilt work at the time!

■ **In Charm School, you learn the social graces. But in Quilter's Charm
School you learn is that** sometimes some of the charm squares are
better suited to go in your stash than in the quilt you are designing. Don't
feel bad for them. They will make all kinds of new friends in the stash!

Three Times a Charm by Sandy Klop

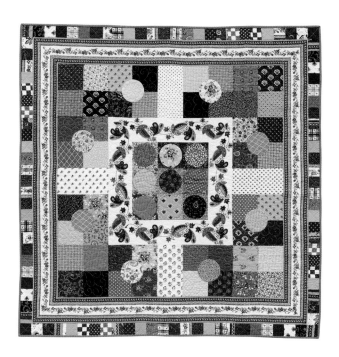

- **FINISHED QUILT:** 52½" × 52½"
- **CHARM PACKS NEEDED:** ■ ■ ■

Bright polka dots dance across the patchwork in this cheerful quilt. To make the eye-catching mitered borders, choose a coordinating border print and fussy cut the sections you like best for your design.

Materials

Yardage is based on 42"-wide fabric. Charm squares are 5" × 5".

3 charm packs of assorted bright and cream prints for quilt top and outer border (you'll need 107 squares, including at least 8 cream squares)

1½ yards of floral border print for borders

½ yard of green print for binding

3½ yards of fabric for backing

59" × 59" piece of batting

Cutting

From *16* of the bright charm squares, cut:
16 rectangles, 4¾" × 5"

From *each of 25* charm squares, cut:
4 squares, 2½ × 2½"

From the border print, cut from the *lengthwise* grain:
4 strips, 4½" × 52"*
4 strips, 4¾" × 26"*

From the green print for binding, cut:
6 strips, 2½" × 42"

*Sandy fussy-cut the border print to center the design motifs within the strips.

Assembling the Quilt Center

Press the seam allowances as indicated by the arrows.

1 Using 17 of the bright 5" squares and the pattern on page 65, prepare 17 circles for appliqué according to your preferred method (see "Appliqué Options" on page 65). Select nine circles for the quilt center, and pair each one with a charm square for the background. Reserve the remaining eight appliqué circles for the quilt top. Appliqué the circles to the nine selected charm squares.

2 Arrange the appliquéd squares in three rows of three. Join the squares in each row, and then join the rows. The center block should measure 14" square, including ¼" seam allowances.

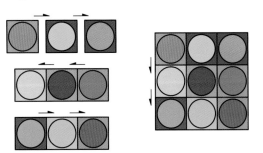

3 Fold the center unit in half vertically and horizontally and pin-mark the centers of the edges. Fold each 4¾" × 26" strip in half and pin-mark the centers. Measuring from the center of each strip, use a pin to mark 7" from both sides of the center.

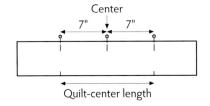

Center
7"   7"
Quilt-center length

4 Pin a strip to the center unit with right sides together, matching the center points. Align the pins at both ends of the strip with the edges of the center unit, and ease the strip to fit. Stitch to the quilt center unit, beginning and ending ¼" from the edges of the center unit. Repeat with the three remaining strips.

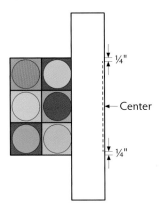

¼"
Center
¼"

5 Lay the first corner to be mitered on an ironing board. Fold under one border strip at a 45° angle to the other strip. Press, and then unfold. Fold the center unit with right sides together, aligning the adjacent edges of the strips. Stitch on the pressed crease, sewing from the previous stitching line to the outer edges.

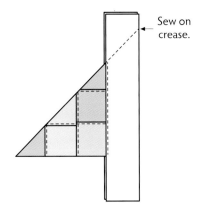

Sew on crease.

6 Press the seam allowances open, check the right side of the quilt to make sure the miters are neat, and then turn the quilt over and trim away the excess border strips, leaving a ¼" seam allowance. Repeat with the remaining corners. The quilt center should measure 22½" square.

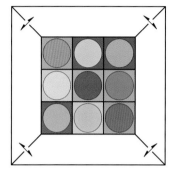

Assembling the Quilt Top

Press the seam allowances as indicated by the arrows.

1 Sew bright charm squares to opposite sides of a cream charm square. Then sew a bright 4¾" × 5" rectangle to each end of the strip, which should measure 5" × 22½".

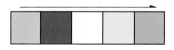

Make 8.

2 Sew two bright charm squares to each end of four of the units from step 1. The units should measure 5" × 40½".

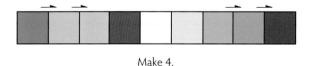

Make 4.

3 Join two of the units from step 1 along the long edges. Repeat with the two remaining units. Sew these units to the sides of the quilt center.

4 Join two of the units from step 2 along the long edges. Repeat with the two remaining units. Sew these units to the top and bottom of the quilt top. The quilt top should measure 40½" square.

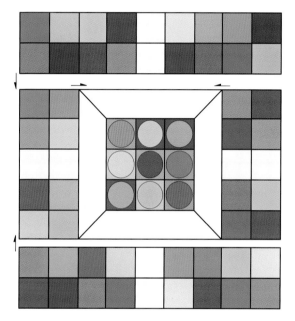

5 Appliqué the remaining eight circles to the quilt top, referring to the photo on page 61 for placement. Center the circles over the seam intersections.

Charmed, I'm Sure!

from **SANDY KLOP**

Sandy Klop charms the quilting world as American Jane (AmericanJane.com).

- **What charms me most about charm packs is** that I don't have to cut them. Such a time-saver!

- **Same or different? If you're making a project with multiple charm packs are you more likely to use two or three of the same collection or from different collections?** Different! The more the merrier.

- **This works like a charm for me every time:** Before you begin cutting, organize your charm pack into lights, darks, and duplicates.

- **About those pinked edges, here's my advice for taking them into account when you sew:** Let them be. Just jump in and start sewing.

- **Besides a 5" charm-square, my other go-to precut shape is** a 10" square.

- **If I taught at Quilters' Finishing School, I'd teach the students to** sing their own song! Don't let anyone tell you otherwise!

- **If I had to pick a "lucky" charm out of a charm pack, I'd choose** any one that gets my attention, good or bad. If it's really good, it can go anywhere. If it's really bad, I'd want to plan where it goes.

- **In Charm School, you learn the social graces. But in Quilter's Charm School you learn** that a light background can show off the darks (or the reverse).

Adding the Borders

Press the seam allowances as indicated by the arrows.

1 Use the floral 4½" × 52" strips to make and attach a mitered border to the outer edges of the quilt top in the same manner as the mitered border of the quilt center. The quilt top should measure 48½" square.

2 Join 24 assorted 2½" squares. The unit should measure 2½" × 48½". Make two. Sew these units to the sides of the quilt top. Join 26 assorted 2½" squares. The unit should measure 2½" × 52½". Make two. Sew these units to the top and bottom of the quilt. The quilt should measure 52½" square.

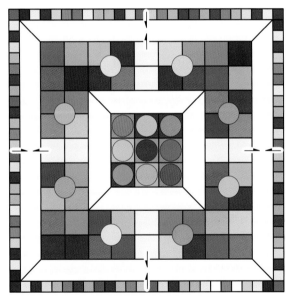

Quilt assembly

Finishing the Quilt

Go to ShopMartingale.com/HowtoQuilt for more details on quilting and finishing.

1 Layer the backing, batting, and quilt top; baste the layers together. Hand or machine quilt as desired. The quilt shown was machine quilted with a swirl and flower design in the background. The center border is quilted with a feather design, and the outer pieced border has an X quilted in each square.

2 Use the green 2½"-wide strips to make the binding and attach it to the quilt.

APPLIQUÉ OPTIONS

This design features 17 appliquéd circles. Sandy used needle-turn appliqué to attach the circles to her quilt, but you can use whatever technique you prefer. For information and instructions for various appliqué methods, go to ShopMartingale.com/HowtoQuilt.

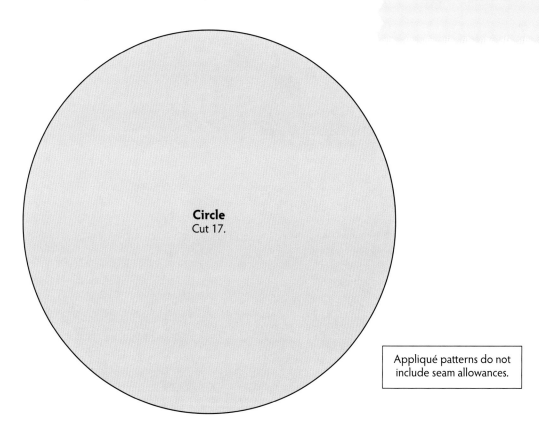

Circle
Cut 17.

Appliqué patterns do not include seam allowances.

Tire Tracks

by Carrie Nelson and Tammy Vonderschmitt

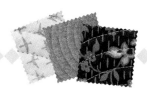

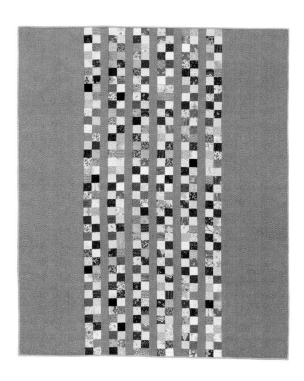

- FINISHED QUILT: 57¾" × 70½"
- CHARM PACKS NEEDED: ▪ ▪ ▪

Simplicity in both the layout and color palette gives this easy quilt its gentle beauty. The scrappy pieced rows are balanced by faded red cross-weave cotton that adds subtle texture. The blue striped binding adds a special finishing touch.

Materials

Yardage is based on 42"-wide fabric. Charm squares are 5" × 5".

3 charm packs of assorted blue, beige, and cream prints for pieced strips (you'll need 120 squares)
2⅛ yards of red cross-weave cotton for background
⅝ yard of blue stripe for binding
4¾ yards of fabric for backing
64" × 77" piece of batting

Cutting

From *each* of 120 charm squares, cut:
4 squares, 2¼" × 2¼" (480 total)

From the pink cross-weave cotton, cut from the *lengthwise* grain:
2 strips, 14¼" × 70½"
5 strips, 2¼" × 70½"

From the blue stripe, cut:
7 strips, 2½" × 42"

Charmed, I'm Sure!

from **CARRIE NELSON**

Now that Carrie Nelson has moved to Moda Fabrics' hometown of Dallas, Texas, she's kicking up her heels in cowboy boots and working on her Southern charm.

- **What charms me most about charm packs is the** variety! Fat quarters are so "yesterday." With charm packs, I can mix so many more collections, colors, and styles of fabric.

- **Same or different? If you're making a project with multiple charm packs, are you more likely to use two or three of the same collection or from different collections?** Different.

- **This works like a charm for me every time:** Sizing or starch prep. It works like prewashing with the benefit of crisping up the fabric.

- **About those pinked edges, here's my advice for taking them into account when you sew:** Wait for it . . . it depends. For accurate piecing, cut them off. For anything where you'll be trimming after piecing or making subcuts, leave them be for now.

- **Besides a 5" charm square, my other go-to precut shape is** . . . It's all about the cake—Layer Cakes! 10" x 10" squares.

- **If I taught at Quilters' Finishing School, I'd teach the students to** experiment! It's fabric, not brain surgery. Have fun, make mistakes, and don't worry about what anybody else thinks. And don't forget to add a label.

- **If I had to pick a "lucky" charm out of a charm pack, I'd choose** a medium-scale text print, preferably in a color on a cream or ivory background. I am a girl who likes words . . . lol.

Assembling the Pieced Strips

Press the seam allowances as indicated by the arrows or as instructed below.

Join 40 squares; press the seam allowances open or in one direction. The pieced strips should measure 2¼" × 70½". Make 12. Join two pieced strips along the long edge. The pieced strip should measure 4" × 70½". Make six pieced strips.

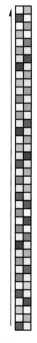

Make 6 rows,
4" × 70½".

Assembling the Quilt Top

Press the seam allowances as indicated by the arrows. Lay out the pieced strips, 2¼"-wide red strips, and 14¼"-wide red strips in vertical rows as shown. Join the red strips and pieced strips; press. The quilt top should measure 57¾" × 70½".

Finishing the Quilt

Go to ShopMartingale.com/HowtoQuilt for more details on quilting and finishing.

1 Layer the backing, batting, and quilt top; baste the layers together. Hand or machine quilt as desired. The quilt shown was machine quilted with a swirl and flower design in the background and with an allover Baptist fan pattern as a counterpoint to the many squares and right angles in the quilt.

2 Use the blue 2½"-wide strips to make the binding and attach it to the quilt.

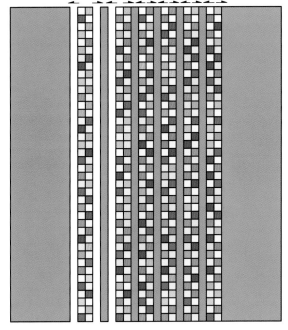

Quilt assembly

Spinning Tops by Jen Kingwell

- **FINISHED SIZE:** 21" × 26¼" (fits a standard bed pillow)
- **FINISHED HEXAGON:** Length of 1 side is 2⅝"; approximate height is 4⅜" (flat edge to flat edge)
- **CHARM PACKS NEEDED:** ■ ■ ■

Select three charm packs with a combination of bright and neutral prints to make a showstopping pillow cover that will brighten any seat or bedroom in the house. Jen hand pieced the intricate blocks for accuracy, but you can piece them by machine if you prefer.

Materials

Charm squares are 5" × 5".

2 charm packs (77 pieces) of polka dots (called "bright") for hexagons and pieced pillow back

1 charm pack (30 pieces) of geometric prints (called "neutral") for hexagons, background, and pillow back

1 strip of tan polka dot, 2" × 21½", for pillow back

Template plastic

21"-long gray or taupe polyester zipper

Cutting

Use the patterns on page 77 and refer to the cutting layout below to cut the hexagon pieces from template plastic. Transfer all dots to the fabric pieces.

From the bright charm squares, cut:

32 hexagons
92 small triangles

From the neutral charm squares, cut:

14 large triangles
92 small triangles

Cutting layout

Piecing the Hexagons

Press the seam allowances as indicated by the arrows. The front panel contains 28 blocks and four half blocks. For each block, select one hexagon, three neutral small triangles, and three bright small triangles. For each half block, select one hexagon, two neutral small triangles, and two bright triangles.

1 Place a neutral small triangle on the top edge of a hexagon with right sides together. Sew a partial seam along the hexagon upper edge between the marked dots as shown.

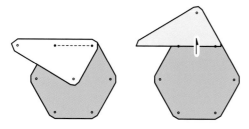

2 Working clockwise, sew a polka dot small triangle to the adjacent edge of the hexagon as shown. The blocks will eventually be joined using a Y-seam, so it's necessary to leave ¼" unstitched beyond the marked dots.

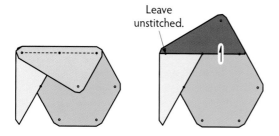

Leave unstitched.

3 Sew the remaining small triangles to the hexagon as shown and complete the seam of the first triangle.

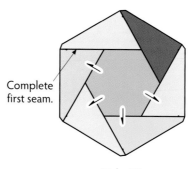

Complete first seam.

Make 28.

4 To make a left half block, sew two neutral and two bright small triangles to one hexagon as shown. Trim the block, leaving a ¼" seam allowance along the left edge. Make two.

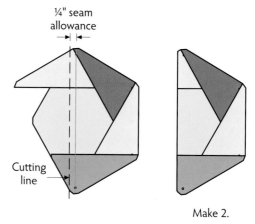

¼" seam allowance

Cutting line

Make 2.

5 To make a right half block, sew two neutral and two bright small triangles to one hexagon, working *counterclockwise* as shown. Trim the block, leaving a ¼" seam allowance along the right edge. Make two.

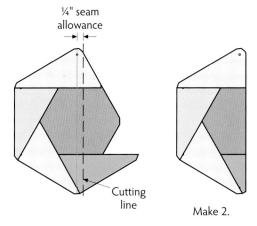

¼" seam
allowance

Cutting
line

Make 2.

BY HAND

*To make this project
portable, hand piece the
hexagons like Jen did.
Cut out the pieces and then
pack them in a project bag
to take on the go.*

Assembling the Front Panel

Press the seam allowances as indicated by the arrows.

1 Lay out the blocks in five rows as shown. Fill in the sides with the right and left half blocks. Make sure the orientation of all blocks is the same in order to complete the pattern. Join the blocks in each row, sewing only between the marked dots.

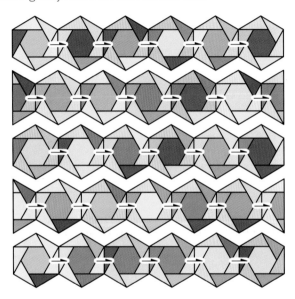

2 When joining the rows, the intersections of the blocks require sewing Y-seams. Place the rows with right sides together. Sew the blocks between the marked dots, and then pivot the fabric to align the adjacent edges and sew between the next set of dots.

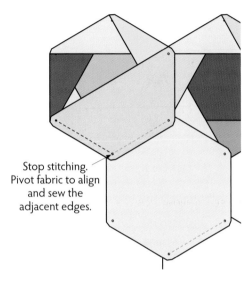

Stop stitching. Pivot fabric to align and sew the adjacent edges.

3 Press the seam allowances open to reduce bulk at the intersections.

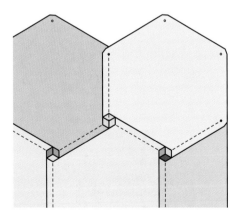

4 Fill in the top and bottom edges of the front panel with the large triangles. Sew the triangles to the top and bottom edges using Y-seams as shown in step 2. When complete, trim the edges of the triangles even with the edges of the front panel. The panel should measure approximately 21½" × 26¾".

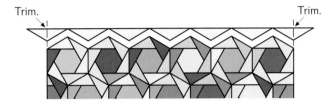

Assembling the Back

Press the seam allowances as indicated by the arrows. The back consists of two panels made from 30 of the remaining charm squares, one fabric strip, and a zipper.

1 Join five of the remaining charm squares to create a pieced strip. Reserve the strip for step 4.

2 Lay out five rows of five charm squares. Join the blocks in each row, and then join the rows.

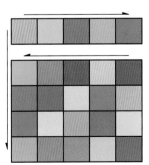

3 Fold the tan fabric strip in half lengthwise with wrong sides together; press. Lay the pieced square right side up. Place the folded strip along one edge of the rectangle, aligning the raw edges. Place the zipper right side down on the strip, flush with the right edge of the rectangle as shown; pin. Using a zipper foot, sew through all three layers close to the zipper teeth.

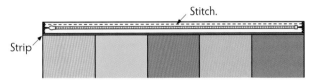

4 Press the strip away from the pieced square. The strip will now conceal the zipper.

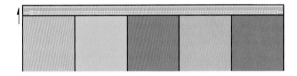

5 Fold the tan strip out of the way, and place the pieced strip from step 1 right side down over the free edge of the zipper; pin. Sew close to the zipper teeth, and then press. Trim the back panel to measure 21½" × 26¾".

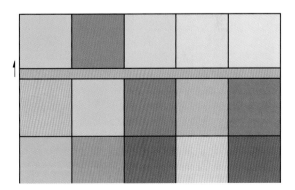

Charmed, I'm Sure!

from JEN KINGWELL

Jen Kingwell (JenKingwellDesigns.blogspot.com) is a real chah-mer, which is to say she's an Aussie charmer with a delightful Aussie accent!

- **What charms me most about charm packs is** the scrappy quilts I can create from a collection of them.

- **Same or different? If you're making a project with multiple charm packs, are you more likely to use two or three of the same collection or from different collections?** Different.

- **This works like a charm for me every time:** Always saying, "I'm on a deadline," so my husband cooks dinner!

- **About those pinked edges, here's my advice for taking them into account when you sew:** They always end up in the bin (wastebasket) as I cut up my charm squares.

- **Besides a 5" charm-square, my other go-to precut shape is** a 10" square. We roll them up and call them lollies in my store. Calorie free!

- **If I taught at Quilters' Finishing School, I'd teach the students** hand quilting. It's my favorite! I definitely know it wouldn't be labels. I never get around to putting those on my quilts!

- **If I had to pick a "lucky" charm out of a charm pack, I'd choose** a good polka dot! I love me a good polka dot. (But you know me, I could never choose only one!)

- **In Charm School, you learn the social graces. But in Quilter's Charm School you learn** to play nicely with lots and lots of others, even if they are the "squares" at Quilter's Charm School.

Assembling the Pillow Cover

Place the front and back panels right sides together; pin. Make sure the zipper is unzipped 3" to 4" to allow the cover to be turned right side out. Sew the perimeter. Clip the corners, and then turn the cover right side out; press.

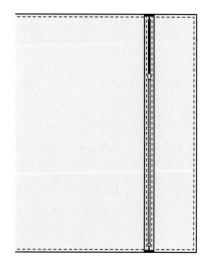

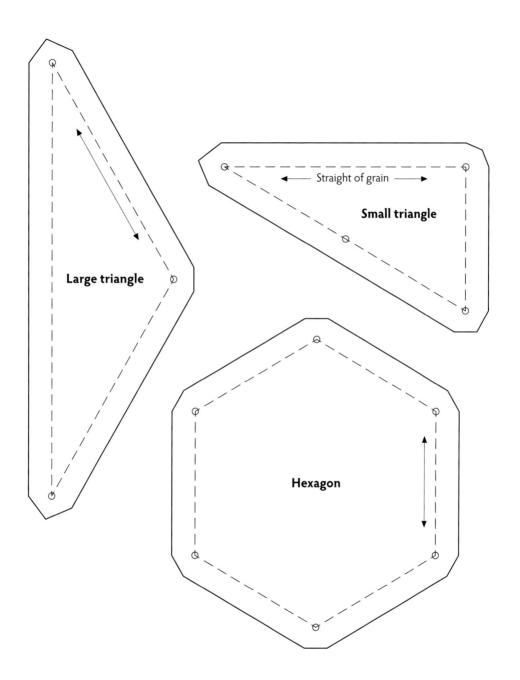

Large triangle

Straight of grain

Small triangle

Hexagon

Beehive
designed by Deb Strain, made by Carol Doolin

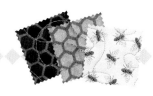

- FINISHED QUILT: 36½" × 51½"
- FINISHED BLOCK: 9" × 9"
- CHARM PACKS NEEDED: ■ ■ ■

Make a quilt that's as sweet as honey from three yellow and black bumblebee-print charm packs. Carry through the theme with a neighborhood of busy beehives alternating with honeycomb rows.

Materials

Yardage is based on 42"-wide fabric. Charm squares are 5" × 5".

3 charm packs of assorted black, yellow, gray, and white bee-themed prints for blocks and rows (you'll need 15 black, 47 yellow, and 48 light squares)
1 yard of black honeycomb print for blocks, rows, and strips
⅓ yard of gold honeycomb print for beehives and binding
2½ yards of fabric for backing
42" × 57" piece of batting
Fusible web

Cutting

All measurements include ¼"-wide seam allowances.

From *each of 32* yellow charm squares, cut:
4 squares, 2" × 2" (128 total)

From *each* of 15 black and 15 yellow charm squares, cut:
2 rectangles, 1¾" × 5" (60 total)

From the black honeycomb print, cut:
4 strips, 2½" × 36½"
32 rectangles, 4½" × 5"

From the gold honeycomb print, cut:
5 strips, 2½" × 42"

Assembling the Honeycomb Rows

Press the seam allowances as indicated by the arrows.

1 Draw a diagonal line from corner to corner on the wrong side of the yellow 2" squares. Place one square on each corner of a black rectangle with right sides together. Sew on the drawn lines. Trim the yellow squares ¼" from the line; press. Make 32.

 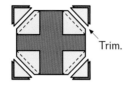

Trim.

Make 32.

2 Join eight Honeycomb blocks in a row, sewing them along their 4½" edges. The row should measure 4½" × 36½". Make four.

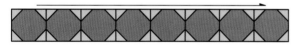

Make 4 rows, 4½" × 36½".

Assembling the Beehive Blocks

Press the seam allowances as indicated by the arrows.

1 Select 48 light charm squares. Lay out two rows of two squares. Join the squares in each row, and then join the rows to make a Four Patch block. The block should measure 9½" square. Make 12.

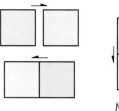

Make 12 blocks,
9½" × 9½".

2 Join five black and yellow 1¾" × 5" rectangles along the long edges; press. Using the pattern on page 83, trace a beehive onto the paper side of the fusible web, and then roughly cut it out. Fuse the beehive to the wrong side of the pieced panel. Cut out the beehive along the traced lines. Make an appliqué door using the pattern on page 83 and the leftover charm pack scraps. Fuse the beehive and door onto one of the blocks from step 1 as shown, and then blanket stitch the edges. Repeat to make 12 beehives and appliqué each to a Four Patch block.

Make 12.

3 Join four Beehive blocks side by side. The row should measure 9½" × 36½". Make three Beehive rows.

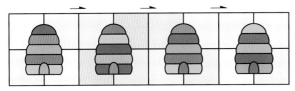

Make 3 rows, 9½" × 36½".

Assembling the Quilt Top

Press the seam allowances as indicated by the arrows. Lay out the Honeycomb rows, Beehive rows, and black strips as shown. Join the rows and strips; press. The quilt should measure 36½" × 51½".

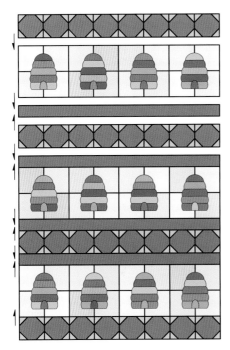

Quilt assembly

Charmed, I'm Sure!

from **DEB STRAIN**

Deb Strain (Facebook.com/DebStrainStudio) is as charming in person as her quilts are!

- **What charms me most about charm packs is** that I can see the entire fabric collection at a glance. And, having downsized our home, charm packs are nice because they don't take up a lot of space!

- **Same or different? If you're making a project with multiple charm packs, are you more likely to use two or three of the same collection or from different collections?** Same.

- **This works like a charm for me every time:** I have a glass of wine in the evening as I'm picking out the color combinations. It helps me relax and not rush the process of putting colors and patterns together. Great way to spend an evening!

- **About those pinked edges, here's my advice for taking them into account when you sew:** I just pretend they aren't there and each edge is a straight cut. When I was little, Mom had me pink every edge, so this seems pretty natural to me.

- **Besides a 5" charm-square, my other go-to precut shape is** a 10" Layer Cake square. I paint all my fabric designs by hand. A Layer Cake seems like 42 pieces of 10" x 10" finished artwork to me! Oh, so many possibilities!

- **If I had to pick a "lucky" charm out of a charm pack, I'd choose** one that had a monotone swirly pattern on it that would work well with simpler or more complicated patterns.

- **In Charm School, you learn the social graces. But in Quilter's Charm School you learn** that it's all about color and color combinations, using warm and cool colors to make one pop, or colors of the same value to make them blend. Colors can add dimension and interest, simply by how they are used together.

Finishing the Quilt

Go to ShopMartingale.com/HowtoQuilt for more details on quilting and finishing.

1. Layer the backing, batting, and quilt top; baste the layers together. Hand or machine quilt as desired. The quilt shown was machine quilted with an allover swirl and loop design.

2. Use the yellow 2½"-wide strips to make the binding and attach it to the quilt.

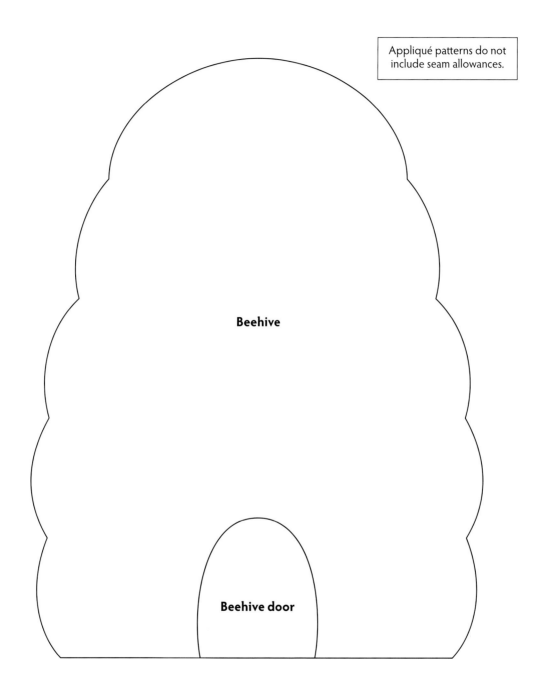

Appliqué patterns do not include seam allowances.

Beehive

Beehive door

Flying Geese by Bonnie Olaveson

- **FINISHED QUILT: 51½" × 57½"**
- **FINISHED BLOCK: 6" × 6"**
- **CHARM PACKS NEEDED: ■ ■ ■**

Make a fanciful flock of geese flying every which way. Combine a variety of printed charm squares with a white background to add cohesion.

Materials

Yardage is based on 44"-wide fabric. Charm squares are 5" × 5".

3 charm packs of assorted bright prints for blocks
  (you'll need 108 squares)
3½ yards of white solid for background
½ yard of red print for binding
3¼ yards of fabric for backing
58" × 64" piece of batting

Cutting

All measurements include ¼"-wide seam allowances.

From the charm squares, cut:
216 rectangles, 2½" × 4½"

From the white solid, cut:
6 strips, 2" × 42"
6 strips, 6½" × 42"; crosscut into 144 rectangles,
  1½" × 6½"
27 strips, 2½" × 42"; crosscut into 432 squares,
  2½" × 2½"

From the red print, cut:
6 strips, 2½" × 42"

Assembling the Blocks

Press the seam allowances indicated by the arrows.

1 Draw a diagonal line from corner to corner on the wrong side of the white squares. Place one square on one end of a print rectangle. Sew on the line, and then trim ¼" from the seam. Press.

2 Sew a white square to the opposite end of the rectangle with the diagonal running in the opposite direction to make a flying-geese unit. Press. Repeat to make a total of 216 flying-geese units.

Make 216 units,
2½" × 4½".

3 Join the three flying geese units along the long edges as shown. Sew white 1½" × 6½" rectangles to the sides of the unit. The block should measure 6½" square. Make 72 blocks.

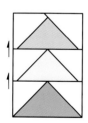 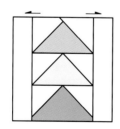

Make 72 blocks,
6½" × 6½".

Assembling the Quilt Top

Press the seam allowances as indicated by the arrows.

1 Lay out the blocks in eight vertical rows of nine as shown, alternating the direction of the flying geese from block to block. Join the blocks in each row, and then join the rows; press. The quilt center should measure 48½" × 54½".

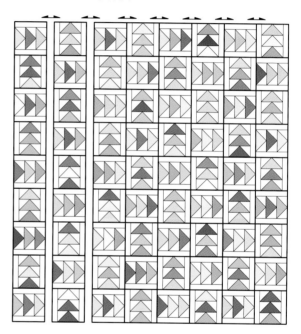

Quilt assembly

2 Join the 2"-wide white strips end to end; press the seam allowances open. Cut two strips, 48½" long. Sew the strips to the top and bottom of the quilt; press the seam allowances toward the strips. Cut two strips to fit the length of the quilt, which should be 57½". Sew the strips to the sides of the quilt; press. The quilt should measure 51½" × 57½".

Finishing the Quilt

For more details on quilting and finishing, you can visit ShopMartingale.com/HowtoQuilt.

1 Layer the backing, batting, and quilt top; baste the layers together. Hand or machine quilt as desired. The quilt shown was machine quilted with an allover swirl design.

2 Use the red 2½"-wide strips to make the binding and attach it to the quilt.

Charmed, I'm Sure!

from **BONNIE OLAVESON**

Bonnie Olaveson has oodles of charm! She's not only the genius behind Cotton Way (Facebook.com/Bonnie.Cotton.Way), she's half of the Moda fabric design team of Bonnie & Camille.

- **What charms me most about charm packs is** that I love having one of every print in the line. It makes projects look so scrappy, and scrappy quilts are my favorite.

- **Same or different? If you're making a project with multiple charm packs, are you more likely to use two or three of the same collection or from different collections?** Different.

- **This works like a charm for me every time:** Chocolate. I call it my vitamin C. C is for creativity. I never start my creating process without a little chocolate close by. As for a quilt tip, press each seam after it's sewn. I think this is a very important part of getting a good result. I love my steam iron and couldn't piece without it.

- **About those pinked edges, here's my advice for taking them into account when you sew:** I like to trim them off to make my measuring and piecing a little more accurate. When I don't, my seams vary more.

- **Besides a 5" charm-square, my other go-to precut shape is** a fat quarter. I love fat quarters!

- **If I taught at Quilters' Finishing School, I'd teach the students to** press their binding after it is hand stitched to the back. Maybe I'm old school, but I love how nice a pressed binding looks.

- **If I had to pick a "lucky" charm out of a charm pack, I'd choose** one that's red with a small white dot. It's the one I choose first every time!

- **In Charm School, you learn the social graces. But in Quilter's Charm School you learn** contrast. I personally love high contrast, so I place fabrics together that have good contrast. That way, the design of the quilt is very obvious. Generally, I pull out the charms that are too blendy with the background fabric.

Little Village, Big Woods by Janet Clare

- **FINISHED QUILT:** 54½" × 54½"
- **CHARM PACKS NEEDED:** ■ ■ ■

Appliqué a quaint country village nestled within a forest of oak and pine trees. Use three charm packs in soft shades of green, dusty blue, and navy for the quick-to-piece patchwork borders.

Materials

Yardage is based on 42"-wide fabric. Charm squares are 5" × 5".

3 charm packs of assorted cream, navy, green, and dusty blue prints for borders (you'll need 114 squares)
½ yard of indigo tone on tone for appliqué
1⅜ yards of cream tone on tone for background
½ yard of dusty blue tone on tone for binding
3½ yards of fabric for backing
61" × 61" piece of batting
1 yard of fusible web (for fusible appliqué only)
Indigo embroidery floss and needle (optional)

Cutting

From *each* charm square, cut:
2 rectangles, 2½" × 5" (228 total)

From the cream tone on tone, cut:
2 strips, 6½" × 38½"
2 strips, 6½" × 26½"
1 square, 18½" × 18½"

From the dusty blue print, cut:
6 strips, 2½" × 42"

Appliquéing the Quilt Center and Border

Janet used fusible appliqué for the quilt shown. For more detailed instructions on fusible appliqué, go to ShopMartingale.com/HowtoQuilt.

1 Using the indigo fabric and the templates on pages 93 and 94, prepare the appliqué pieces for fusible appliqué according to your preferred method (see "Appliqué Options" below left). For fusible appliqué, trace the pieces onto the paper side of the fusible web. The quilt center includes the following pieces.

- 1 church
- 1 windmill
- 2 barns (1 with barn roof A and 1 with barn roof B)
- 2 house A (1 with house roof A and 1 with house roof B)
- 1 house B
- 18 oak trees (3 are for the quilt center)
- 33 pine trees (5 are for the quilt center)
- 3 fences
- 3 birds

2 Refer to the photo on page 89 for placing the appliqués on the 18½" cream square. Fuse the appliqués in place, and then stitch the edges using Janet's machine-drawing technique or the stitch of your choosing (or attach the appliqués according to your preferred method). If desired, hand embroider a cross on top of the church steeple using a backstitch and two strands of embroidery floss.

APPLIQUÉ OPTIONS

Janet used fusible appliqué for her quilt, so the patterns on pages 93 and 94 have been reversed. After fusing the pieces in place, she used matching thread and a straight stitch to sew ⅛" from the edges. She used her "machine drawing" technique, in which she lowers the feed dogs on her machine to free-motion stitch around the edge of each shape.

3 Janet used a random assortment of oak and pine trees for each border to give the sense of a forest surrounding the village. Refer to the photo on page 89 for inspiration and for the placement of the trees. Appliqué the trees to the cream strips.

Assembling the Pieced Borders

Press the seam allowances as indicated by the arrows.

1 For the inner pieced border, join nine print rectangles along the long edges. The unit should measure 18½" long. Make two. Join 13 rectangles along the long edges. The unit should measure 26½" long. Make two. Trim all of the units to measure 4½" wide.

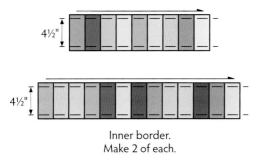

Inner border.
Make 2 of each.

2 For the first outer pieced border, join 19 print rectangles along the long edges. The unit should measure 38½" long. Make two. Join 23 rectangles along the long edges. The unit should measure 46½" long. Make two. Trim all of the units to measure 4½" wide.

3 For the second outer pieced border, join 23 print rectangles along the long edges. The unit should measure 46½" long. Make two. Join 27 rectangles along the long edges. The unit should measure 54½" long. Make two. Trim all of the units to measure 4½" wide.

Assembling the Quilt Top

Press the seam allowances as indicated by the arrows. Sew the short inner pieced borders to the top and bottom of the quilt center. Sew the long inner pieced borders to the sides of the quilt center. Repeat to sew the cream border and outer pieced borders to the quilt center in the same manner as shown in the quilt assembly diagram.

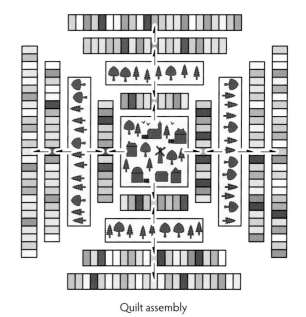

Quilt assembly

Charmed, I'm Sure!

from JANET CLARE

Janet Clare (JanetClare.co.uk) brings a hint of royalty to the group with her English charm. Cheerio!

- **What charms me most about charm packs is that** the 5" size is my favorite size of square.

- **Same or different? If you're making a project with multiple charm packs, are you more likely to use two or three of the same collection or from different collections?** Same.

- **This works like a charm for me every time:** Always press seam allowances open.

- **About those pinked edges, here's my advice for taking them into account when you sew:** I measure and stitch from the outside of the pinked edge and don't worry about them after that!

- **Besides a 5" charm-square, my other go-to precut shape is a** Jelly Roll of 2½" strips.

- **If I taught at Quilters' Finishing School, I'd teach the students to** make a note of the date they started the quilt and the date they finished it. These are often quite far apart in my experience! Then stitch a really lovely quilt label adding these dates and as much other information as you can, along with a personal message. Quilts are heirlooms, and your family will want to know these things in the years ahead.

- **If I had to pick a "lucky" charm out of a charm pack, I'd choose** a small-scale blender print because they are the most versatile.

- **In Charm School, you learn the social graces. But in Quilter's Charm School you learn** there's always one that doesn't quite fit, so set it aside until you find the perfect use for it.

Finishing the Quilt

For more details on quilting and finishing, you can visit ShopMartingale.com/HowtoQuilt.

1. Layer the backing, batting, and quilt top; baste the layers together. Hand or machine quilt as desired. The quilt shown was machine quilted with a swirl and flower design in the background and with outline quilting in the border.

2. Use the blue 2½"-wide strips to make the binding and attach it to the quilt.

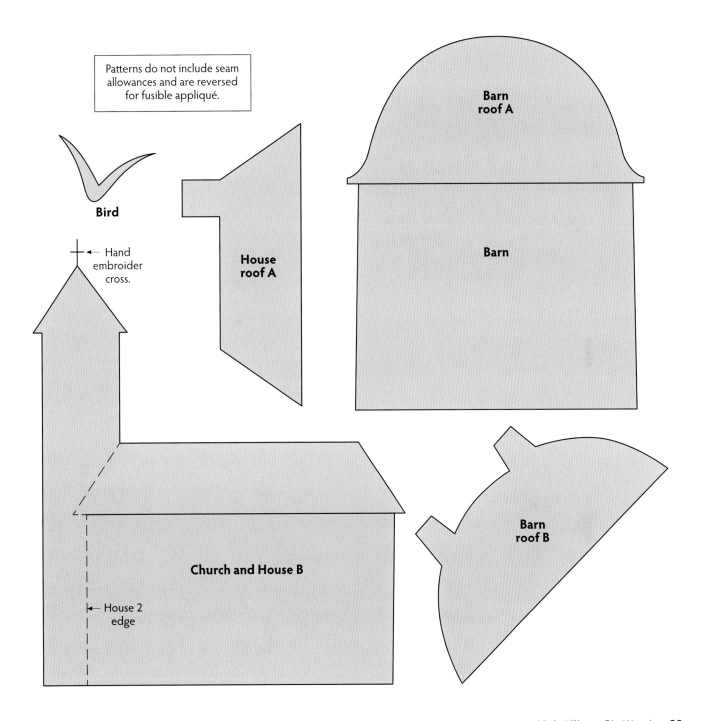

Patterns do not include seam allowances and are reversed for fusible appliqué.

Bird

Hand embroider cross.

House roof A

Barn roof A

Barn

Church and House B

House 2 edge

Barn roof B

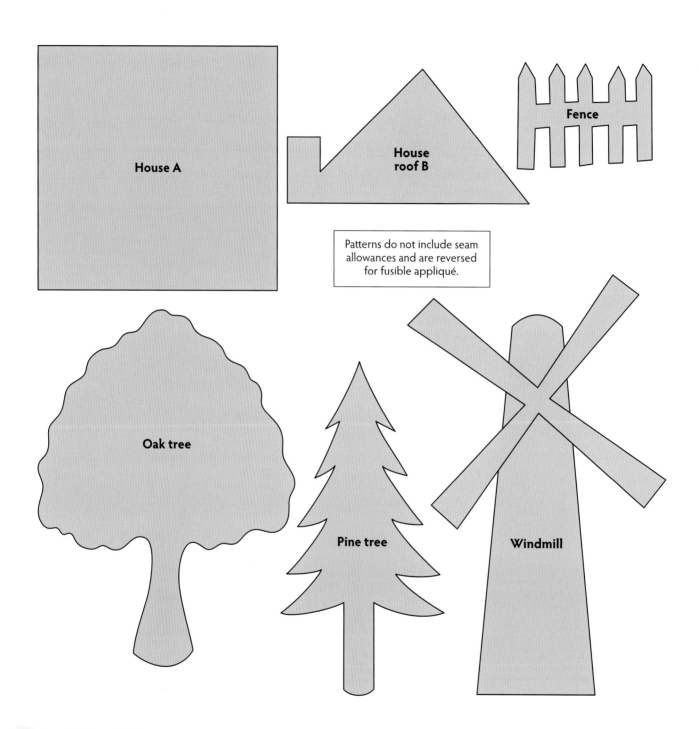

House A

House roof B

Fence

Patterns do not include seam allowances and are reversed for fusible appliqué.

Oak tree

Pine tree

Windmill

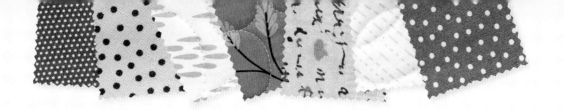

Meet the Contributors

Lissa Alexander
ModaLissa.blogspot.com

Lisa Bongean
LisaBongean.com

Janet Clare
JanetClare.co.uk

Jenny Doan
MissouriQuiltCo.com

Karla Eisenach
TheSweetwaterCo.com

Sandy Gervais
PiecesfromMyHeart.net

**Barbara Groves and
Mary Jacobson**
MeandMySisterDesigns.com

Lynne Hagmeier
KTQuilts.com

Jen Kingwell
JenKingwellDesigns.blogspot.com

Sandy Klop
AmericanJane.com

Sherri McConnell
AQuiltingLife.com

Carrie Nelson
Blog.ModaFabrics.com

Bonnie Olaveson
Facebook.com/Bonnie.Cotton.Way

Kathy Schmitz
KathySchmitz.com

Laurie Simpson
MinickandSimpson.blogspot.com

Pat Sloan
PatSloan.com

Deb Strain
Facebook.com/DebStrainStudio

Anne Sutton
BunnyHillDesigns.com

Discover more fabulous quilt patterns
by your favorite Moda designers

Explore all the inspiring books in the Moda All-Stars series, where you'll discover fresh takes on classic blocks, innovative how-to tips, and clever settings that will make the fabric you love shine. Try a different technique, learn a new sewing trick, and get inspired to make a beautiful quilt today!

Find them all at your local quilt shop or online at ShopMartingale.com

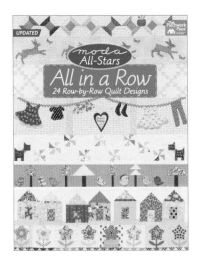
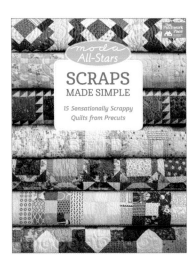